PART-TIME

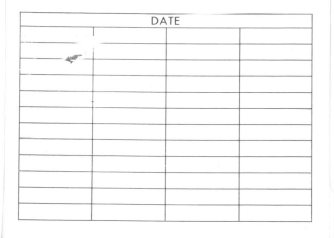

DATE			

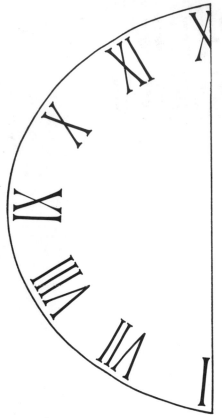

- **Where to Find Part-Time Professional Jobs**

- **Converting Full-Time Positions to Part Time**

- **How to Negotiate with Employers, New and Old**

- **How to Sell Yourself as a Part-Time Worker**

- **Benefits for Part-Time Workers**

- **Professional Advancement on Schedule**

PART-TIME
PROFESSIONAL

by Diane S. Rothberg & Barbara Ensor Cook

ACROPOLIS BOOKS LTD.
WASHINGTON, D.C.

ACROPOLIS BOOKS, LTD.

Colortone Building, 2400 17th St., N.W., Washington, D.C. 20009

Printed in the United States of America by

COLORTONE PRESS, Creative Graphics, Inc., Washington, D.C. 20009

Attention: Schools and Corporations

ACROPOLIS books are available at quantity discounts with bulk purchase for educational, business, or sales promotional use. For information, please write to: SPECIAL SALES DEPARTMENT, ACROPOLIS BOOKS LTD., 2400 17th ST., N.W., WASHINGTON, D.C. 20009

**Are there Acropolis Books you want
but cannot find in your local stores?**

You can get any Acropolis book title in print. Simply send title and retail price, plus $1.00 per copy to cover mailing and handling costs for each book desired. District of Columbia residents add applicable sales tax. Enclose check or money order only, no cash please, to:

ACROPOLIS BOOKS LTD.,

2400 17th St., N.W., WASHINGTON, D.C. 20009

Library of Congress Cataloging in Publication Data

Rothberg, Diane, 1930–
   Part-time professional.

   Includes index.
   1. Part-time employment—United States—Addresses, essays, lectures. 2. Professions—United States—Addresses, essays, lectures.   I. Cook, Barbara, 1950–
II. Title.
HD5110.2.U5R67   1985   650.1'4   85-19964
ISBN 0-87491-786-7

Table of Contents

Introduction

Self-confidence and optimism are crucial for successful job hunting. Unfortunately, many prospective part-time professionals lack these essential ingredients for success. The reason— a total lack of information about the world of part-time professional work.

This book provides the information you need if you wish to pursue a career *and* work fewer hours weekly. Using this book, you can build the self-confidence necessary to translate your dream of a part-time professional position into reality. Many people, even professionals, think that job hunting is looking for published vacancies in local newspapers. Entering the world of part-time professional work requires you to do much more.

First, you must convince yourself that using your professional skills part time is a feasible goal. Unless you believe that this goal is a practical possibility, you cannot sell the idea to an employer. Our book dispels the misconception that part-time professional employment is an illusion by offering a number of examples of professionals on reduced work schedules and companies using part-time professionals. We place these specific profiles of part-timers and employers into a broad national context through a summary of the occupational distribution and total numbers of part-time professionals working today.

You must also understand employers' reactions to part-time professionals. Employers' attitudes are complex, a mixture of positive and negative. Unless you are informed about employers' views, you cannot market yourself as a part-timer capable of solving an employer's problems. Through this book, you will learn how to present to an employer the advantages of using part-time professionals and how to answer any of his or her objections to part-time work.

Since part-time professional employment is a novel idea for many employers, standard job search strategies cannot prepare you adequately for job hunting as a part-timer. You must know about the unique ways to use your skills part time. We show you how to convert your current full-time job to part time; how to locate existing part-time vacancies; how to use full-time jobs as leads; and how to create part-time professional positions. Strategies differ, depending on whether you are already working for an organization or are trying to break in as an outsider. We explore all details, including specifics on negotiating with an employer.

As you job hunt, you must distinguish between private sector employers and government agencies as potential users of your services. Our advice is to explore carefully and systematically the possibilities for part time in private firms, in nonprofit organizations, and in government agencies at all levels. Although our book concentrates on part-time professional employment in the private sector, we describe the special character of government employment and the opportunities available for part-time professionals.

Finally, you must anticipate the problems, as well as the pleasures, of holding a part-time professional job. Appreciating the potential problems leads to prevention. We alert you to these problems so you can prevent them before they emerge or solve them when they occur.

Our years with the Association of Part-Time Professionals have led us to conclude that solid information and guidance empowers qualified professionals to achieve part-time status. Very often, we have found, men and women with excellent training and experience are completely lost when they want to move to reduced work schedules. Our aim, with this book, is to close the knowledge gap.

Be sure we agree on the meaning of the term "part time." We are writing about permanent, not temporary, work. This is an important distinction that prospective part-timers and employers often overlook. How to obtain temporary, or project-specific work, is not covered here. We do not describe strategies for consultants, free-lancers, or contract personnel. While we recognize that employers who use professionals on temporary assignments may be good prospects for part-timers, this book talks solely to the professional who wishes to work permanently on a less than full-time schedule.

Professionals work in permanent, part-time jobs for all kinds of reasons. For many, a reduced work schedule allows more time for parental responsibilities or answers the need for additional income. Others desire to use their education, skills, and experience or simply wish to have more free time to pursue other interests. Less common reasons for working part time are: transition to a new career or business, attending school, caring for relatives, and physical disability. Whatever your reasons, rest assured that other professionals across the country share them.

Part-time employment is widely used and very workable at the professional level. We have tried to capture and consolidate the information gathered in our years of helping professionals achieve their part-time goals. Of course, we would prefer to talk with you personally and to develop with you an individualized job-hunting strategy. As a substitute, we offer our book—and the detail it contains—to help you find your own way.

Chapter One

You Are
Not Alone

Consider yourself a prospective part-time professional if:

- you are a skilled individual who is qualifed to fill a responsible position requiring at least a college degree or its work equivalent, *and*

- you are seeking a regularly scheduled work week of sixteen to thirty-two hours.

A Decade of Growth

Today, over two million men and women choose to work as part-time professionals. Over the past decade, the number of voluntary part-time positions in professional fields has grown by over fifty percent.

Table 1.
On Voluntary Part Time in
Professional, Technical, Managerial,
Administrative Occupations
(thousands)

1972	1,548
1977	1,902
1982	2,363
1984	2,373

You do not have to be an employment expert to know that more women than men prefer part-time hours. Although national figures reinforce the popular perception of part-timers as overwhelmingly female, it is incorrect to view reduced work schedules as exclusively a woman's issue. We believe that, in the near future, increasing numbers of male professionals, especially young retirees, will want permanent part-time work.

Table 2.
Men and Women on Voluntary Part Time in
Professional, Technical, Managerial,
Administrative Occupations
(thousands)

	Men	Women
1972	562	986
1977	643	1,257
1982	697	1,666
1984	669	1,703

Occupational Outlook

Let us look at the two-million-plus jobs held by part-time professionals. Note, in the table below, that the professional specialty occupations employ the overwhelming numbers of part-time professionals. Among the professional specialties, over one-half are in just two fields: health assessment and treatment (including nurses) and teachers (below college level). Do not panic if you fail to see your field on this national list. Your professional area may be concealed in the expanding category, "other professional specialties."

Table 3.
Voluntary Part-Time Labor Force
Employed PT
(thousands)

	1983		1984*	
Executive, administrative, managerial........................	—	**564**	—	**562**
Professional specialty occupations........................	—	**1,709**	—	**1,736**
engineers	24	—	24	—
math and computer scientists	12	—	15	—
natural scientists	20	—	18	—
health diagnosing occupations (medical degree required)	50	—	62	—
health assessment and treating	432	—	433	—
teachers, college and university	154	—	141	—
teachers, excluding college and university	477	—	496	—
lawyers and judges	38	—	37	—
other professional specialties	502	—	511	—
Technicians and related support occupations...........	—	**354**	—	**359**
health technologists and technicians	216	—	213	—
engineering and science technicians	61	—	61	—
technicians, except health, engineering and science (includes computer programmers)	76	—	84	—

*The 1984 totals in Tables 1 and 3 are different because Table 1 uses another data base: persons at work in nonfarm occupations on voluntary part-time schedules. These latter figures are preferred for long-term comparisons.

The Association of Part-Time Professionals (a nonprofit membership organization) provides more details on leading occupations for part-time professionals. In the Washington, D.C. metropolitan area, for example, the association's job referral service reports that the following jobs made its "top ten" list every year between 1980 and 1984:

- editor
- librarian
- mental health counselor
- social worker
- teacher
- writer

Other jobs listed among the top ten in three or more years between 1980 and 1984 were:

- accountant
- computer programmer
- graphic artist
- psychologist

Special Characteristics of Part-Time Professional Jobs

The 40-hour work week is a recent occurrence, historically speaking, beginning in the Depression Era of the 1930's. In 1901, the work week was 58.4 hours and, in 1860, a 68-hour work week was common. By the twenty-first century, we may see a standard work week of considerably less than 40 hours.

Today, many employers still assume that work must be accomplished in 40-hour segments. Often, miscellaneous tasks are added needlessly to a job description so that full-time positions can emerge. More flexible, cost-conscious employers recognize that any job can be performed part time. Jobs, after all, are collections of tasks that can be added to or subtracted from. There is nothing fixed about the 40-hour work week.

Although any job can be part time, jobs with certain special characteristics lend themselves particularly well to part-time schedules. Many leading part-time professional occupations, already mentioned above, exhibit these special characteristics:

- Multiple skills required in the same job. One example is an office management position with personnel and accounting functions. The personnel and accounting responsibilities might be performed more effectively by two part-timers.

- Relatively independent or project-oriented positions. These positions allow their incumbents to plan, organize, and carry out their assignments without continual dependence on the needs and schedules of others. Examples are researchers, attorneys, and conference planners.

- Peak work loads. Positions dealing with the public that have heavy business during certain hours of the day can be filled by part-time professionals who work only those hours. Career counselors and librarians are examples.

- High-stress positions where the individual is subject to constant demands. Social workers and teachers fit this category.

- Scarce job skills. Systems analysts and electrical engineers, for example, can take advantage of their highly marketable skills by asking for reduced work schedules.

- Deadlines known weeks or months in advance. The absence of a crisis environment means that work can be planned and managed effectively on a part-time basis. Editorial positions are examples.

- Creativity a key job component. A shorter work week can increase innovation in jobs that require constant creativity. Writers and public relations professionals fall into this category.

Exercise 1:

(a) Describe your current job *or* the job you want.

Job Description_____

_____

_____

(b) Does the job you described show the special characteristics of a part-time professional job? (Check "yes" or "no" below):

☐ yes	☐ no	multiple skills required in the same job?
☐ yes	☐ no	independent, or project-oriented position?
☐ yes	☐ no	peak work loads?
☐ yes	☐ no	high stress?
☐ yes	☐ no	scarce job skills?
☐ yes	☐ no	deadlines known in advance?
☐ yes	☐ no	creativity constantly required?

(c) Where you checked "yes" above, describe and give specific examples of the special characteristics of the job that make it a good prospect for part-time hours.

Can Managers Work Part Time?

Employers often are reluctant to recognize that managers can work effectively part time. They do not take into account the fact that even full-time managers are away for significant periods of time while at conferences and business meetings—yet the work gets done.

A particular style characterizes many successful part-time managers. They engage in extensive two-way communication with their subordinates and regard work as a team effort. They encourage employees to take on additional responsibilities and to maximize their potential. Three examples follow of managers working part time in government and in the nonprofit private sector. Two women are able to combine their management roles with part-time hours. The third admits she is less successful in maintaining a part-time schedule. All three women discuss the pressures part-time managers must, but sometimes cannot, master.

Katherine Tippett
former Group Leader, Family Economics Research Group, Agricultural Research Service, U.S. Department of Agriculture, Hyattsville, MD

Until 1985, Ms. Tippett supervised a research program related to family uses of resources. A part-timer who worked about 24 hours per week, she supervised a staff of fourteen people, mostly scientists and support personnel. In 1974, she converted to part time because of family responsibilities. Promoted to a higher-level position in 1979, she retained her part-time status after making it clear to her supervisor that she would accept the level of responsibility expected but would perform fewer tasks than her full-time predecessor.

Her predecessor had traveled frequently representing the office at meetings. Ms. Tippett cut back on traveling, urging other scientists in the Research Group to take over some of that responsibility. In effect, this lowered her profile and raised theirs, giving them more visibility and a higher level of responsibility than they might have obtained otherwise. This also made her more available to staff despite her part-time status. When she was not in the office or unavailable by phone, a full-time scientist was able to answer questions and make decisions. But Ms. Tippett points out that this is no different from an office that has a full-time leader who is often away at meetings. Somebody is always there to cover the office.

In 1985, Ms. Tippett transferred to a staff position in another agency, still on a part-time basis.

Agnes Leshner
Coordinator of Training and Development, Department of Social Services, Montgomery County, MD

A psychologist, Ms. Leshner performs an ongoing assessment of agency training needs through regular contact with managerial personnel. She labels hers a "program management" rather than a "people management" slot. Originally a full-time position, it was converted to part time before Agnes Leshner assumed it.

Her schedule (five days per week from 8:30 to 12:30 pm) conforms to the requirements of her program management role. She comes in daily, so afternoon callers know they will receive a response to their queries the very next morning. An extremely competent secretary often can field the questions herself. Agnes Leshner offers the following advice to prospective part-time professionals, whether or not they are in managerial slots:

- Be flexible. "I make it a point to be there if something important is happening at 3:30 in the afternoon."

- Be competent and very reliable. "As models, we have to do our jobs better than the average full-time person."

- Be creative and assertive. "Let others know about the special skills you have and your new ideas. Don't just sit back."

- Talk up the value of part-time professionals. After all, why not emphasize a practice that accommodates both employee and employer?

Phyllis Stein
Director of Career Services, Radcliffe College, Cambridge, MA

Ms. Stein converted her full-time position as Director of Career Services at Radcliffe College to a part-time position in June of 1977. Over the years, her part-time status has evolved more toward full time, going from four-fifths time to six-sevenths time. Since all full-time office directors at the college work at least 50 to 60 hours weekly, she notes, her current job is, in effect, "full" time on a 35-to-40-hour-work week schedule. All too often she stays later than the originally planned 3:30 pm.

A counselor-administrator with a master's degree in human development, Phyllis Stein is responsible for running an office that provides career services to over 3,800 women annually. Her staff includes three full-time people, ten part-timers (including students), and one volunteer.

Strongly committed to Radcliffe and to her work as director, she finds trying to jam all the necessary work into a "part-time" schedule makes life "frantic" for her. Other part-timers, she cautions, should not follow her example of working close to full time for part-time pay. A partial solution has been to "delegate as much as possible." "My management style is incredibly democratic," she adds.

Less time to socialize with colleagues and to engage in "important networking" is a definite drawback. She advises a "very open and friendly" manner as one way to compensate for this loss of socializing on the job. As a part-time professional, she feels you have to discipline yourself to leave work behind, to maintain that often elusive balance between work and outside commitments.

Chapter Two

Profiles of Part-Time Professionals

Throughout this book, you will meet part-time professionals in challenging assignments. Note what they do, their job search strategies, and how they handle problems on the job.

Elaine Walter
Director of Personnel Administration,
Onondaga County Personnel Department, NY

Elaine Walter has overall responsibility for administering the county's salary and wage program, orientation and training programs, and fringe benefit rules and information. About ninety percent of Ms. Walter's time is spent on managerial or supervisory duties, directing one of four divisions of the Personnel Department and assisting in setting county policy on the above programs. She supervises four employees.

Work Schedule: T, W, Th, 9:00 am–5:00 pm. During peak times, she also may work some Mondays. "My job is not the same every month," she says. "If I were full time, I would do the same things 'in more depth'. Now I leave some of the depth to others."

Fringe Benefits: Prorated benefits for sick leave, vacation leave, personal leave, and retirement. She has full coverage health insurance, including dependents.

Job-Search Strategy: Elaine Walter converted from full time to part time as director of personnel administration. Before going on a nine-month maternity leave, she proposed the part-time assignment. It was an oral proposal, presented quite "informally" to her boss and it was readily accepted. Reflecting on the reasons for the easy transition to part-time status, Ms. Walter mentions the following circumstances:

1. Someone else in the personnel department previously had requested permission to work part time, so part-time employment was an accepted practice.

2. Her boss is a "very well-regarded person in the labor-relations field." He is "very current" in his thinking and well aware of the fact that many people are "seeking alternative work."

3. Ms. Walter and her boss have excellent personal rapport, combined with a mutual sense of professional respect and easy communication.

Based on her experience in converting to part time, Elaine Walter suggests the following useful strategies:

- Be a productive, responsible full-timer with a reputation for getting things done.

- For a supervisory position, make sure your staff can work independently. Some people just are not comfortable without daily instructions. The three professionals on Ms. Walter's staff have expressed the thought that their enhanced responsibilities are "enriching."

- Tell the employer what projects are to be completed in the next six to twelve months. Go over the details about how the projects will be accomplished. Propose a trial period for a part-time schedule—with evaluation.

Solving Problems on the Job: One problem can be some difficulty meeting with co-workers. With her schedule, Elaine Walter admits, "a lot can happen over the long weekend that was not anticipated when I left on Thursday." This is solved, usually, she says, "by my staff's own good judgment and my being able to be reached by phone when necessary." Also, "I leave extensive notes and messages." But calls at home are not routine, and when the staff does call, it is to relay information. Very seldom is it a question of "what to do?"

Missing scheduled meetings is another problem. She usually sends a staff member to attend or, occasionally, changes her schedule. There is also some "good natured kidding" by peers about her part-time hours. Getting the work done with the help of an excellent staff keeps the comments to a minimum. Some colleagues do not even realize she works part time, and she does not advertise her status at work as the part-time director of personnel administration. She volunteers this information most often in social situations.

Since working part time, she reports, some employees have called about changing their schedules. Two county librarians will be sharing one job, and two female dispatchers in the sheriff's office also are requesting job sharing. The personnel department encourages part-time work. Several years ago, the department particularly recommended it as a money-saving device for the county. Employees came forward to request part time, and, over the years, a number of managers have permitted it. There seems to be more "formal attention" to part time than ever before, claims Elaine Walter.

Barbara Kelley
Librarian, Small Midwestern Consulting Firm

Enjoying full responsibility for a one-person library, Barbara Kelley performs complicated research, retrieving information from computer data bases around the country. Using a network of information sources she has developed over the years, she responds to colleagues' requests for polls on political attitudes or for sales figures on specific consumer products in different cities. Ms. Kelley is "very satisfied" with her part-time position. She values the great freedom she has on the job and the excitement of working in a large metropolitan area.

Work Schedule: T, W, Th, 8:00 am–5:00 pm. Barbara Kelley often works extra hours, for which she receives her regular hourly rate.

Fringe Benefits: Health insurance at her firm is only for full-time personnel. The absence of health benefits is particularly "troublesome" for Barbara Kelley because she needs coverage under a major-medical plan. Several years ago, she purchased individual health insurance, but after four years, the cost had risen 500 percent. In 1984, she switched to a nonprofit organization's group health insurance plan, saving herself about $2,000 per year.

Ms. Kelley does not participate in her firm's pension plan, but she does take part in the profit-sharing option. There are no paid vacations for part-timers. Workers accumulate six holidays after three years' service.

Job Search Strategy: Barbara Kelley describes her story as a typical case of "housewife syndrome." Until age 45, she stayed home with the kids and did the "volunteer bit." A college graduate in home economics, she returned to school for a master's degree in library science. At age 50, she obtained her first paid employment—elementary library research at 15 cents above the minimum wage. Then friends told her about a possible library opening with a small consulting company. There was no official vacancy, but the company was feeling the loss of its former librarian. Impressed by Ms. Kelley's credentials, the firm decided it really needed somebody to provide research materials for the numerous in-house studies it produces.

Barbara Kelley admits she made a "major mistake" during the salary negotiations. When asked about her hourly rate, she mentioned a rather low figure. This seemed a princely sum to her after the minimum wage rate she earned earlier. By 1984, after six years on the job, her hourly rate had risen about two-thirds. It is crucial, she warns, to start with a competitive salary base. Otherwise, you will be catching up forever on compensation. The low salary she initially requested reflected her negative self-evaluation. Part-time professionals must project a more positive image, she suggests.

Based on Barbara Kelley's experience in obtaining a part-time librarian position with a private firm, she recommends these strategies:

1. Have the necessary credentials, especially educational credentials. Even though personal contacts paved the way for her original interview, she "would never have been looked at without the M.L.S." Going back to school, she says, was "the smartest thing I did."

2. Look and act as a professional at all times in the office.

Solving Problems on the Job: Barbara Kelley did not solve the problem of no health benefits on the job. She was forced to go outside the work place to purchase costly individual and then group health insurance. Since 1978, when she started work as a part-time librarian, Ms. Kelley also has wrestled with the issue of full-time colleagues not taking her seriously. Her solution: "Do a professional job, always."

Gradually, the negative attitudes are disappearing. For the first time before her four-week vacation, colleagues started complaining: "What are we going to do without you?" Or, "Nobody can take over for you." New personnel, a record of outstanding work, more people depending on her for research materials—all these changes are combining to produce a new impression of Barbara Kelley as a committed, very accomplished part-time professional.

Lori Buffum
Teaching Associate and Technical Writer, San Antonio, TX

A "confirmed part-timer," Lori Buffum teaches English composition at the University of Texas (San Antonio) and at San Antonio College. About seventy people work for her department at the University of Texas—the vast majority of whom are part-timers who work on a semester contract system.

At one point she was also a writer for a technical publications and printing company, the Morsi Corporation. She wrote, edited, and evaluated computer documentation and coordinated entire projects for the firm. When juggling her part-time professional jobs and family responsibilities became too much, she relinquished her job at the Morsi Corporation, but may return once her teaching is under control.

Work Schedule: M, W, F, 8:00 am–9:00 am at the University of Texas. W, 6:30 pm–9:30 pm at San Antonio College. Ms. Buffum set her own hours at the Morsi Corporation, generally during the regular work week and sometimes at home. Occasionally, she worked evenings to meet deadlines and traveled on day or overnight trips to Houston or Austin.

Fringe Benefits: Lori Buffum does not require employee benefits because of her husband's benefits package. She reports that teaching two classes or more at the University of Texas entitles you to sign up for health and pension benefits.

Job Search Strategy: "Watch for ads that mention part-time or contract work," Lori Buffum advises. She learned about all her teaching and technical writing positions through vacancy announcements in local newspapers. At Morsi, she was originally hired through a newspaper announcement calling for technical writers, draftsmen, and engineers who wanted contract assignments.

By working on routine jobs, Ms. Buffum became well-known in the company and soon heard about an opening in the technical publications department. Since Morsi is a small firm, she marched over to chat with the manager in charge. The two arranged a new contract and Ms. Buffum switched to writing and editing for the publications section.

Based on her ten years of experience in technical writing and on her part-time teaching career, Lori Buffum recommends that part-time professionals apply for jobs that meet their needs and then express interest in taking on the jobs part time.

Solving Problems on the Job: As a new teaching associate, Ms. Buffum feels a lack of advice and structure on how to do the job. Part-time teachers, she believes, are "as qualified" as full-time staff, but they require guidance on teaching philosophy, sound approaches to the students, and the best instructional materials and techniques. Her solution to this problem is ancient: talk extensively with other part-time faculty and learn from them.

Part-time teachers also have problems with issues of pay, prestige, and treatment. Even when part-timers take on the same class load as full-time teachers, their pay is low and they never know whether "they are going to have a job the following semester." Part-timers, Ms. Buffum suggests, can be treated as a "service group" at the university—not as academic professionals. Lori Buffum recognizes that this hostility to part-time teachers exists throughout higher education; in fact, the Modern Language Association deplores the use of part-time instructors. Regardless of such negatives, she describes herself as "very satisfied" with her part-time status.

Dr. John Stone (name changed)
Student Health Physician, a southern university

More free time to pursue other interests was *the* reason for Dr. John Stone's decision to convert to part time. Part time means working a nine-month rather than a twelve-month schedule at the student health department of a large southern university. He takes three months off each summer—the logical time to take leave because fewer students are on campus and the work load is lighter.

Work Schedule: 4½ days per week, 37 weeks per year.

Fringe Benefits: Health and life insurance, sick leave, and prorated retirement benefits.

Job Search Strategy: Before converting to a part-time schedule, Dr. Stone was a supervisor in the student health department, coordinating the services and activities of other professionals. He resigned from these responsibilities to pursue the part-time option. If you are considering conversion to part time, advises Dr. Stone, prepare a careful argument demonstrating savings to the employer. Prove that no loss in productivity will occur. Very often, he remarks, employers do not appreciate that a part-time arrangement will be "of mutual advantage."

Solving Problems on the Job: John Stone frankly admits he could not solve two problems he encountered as a part-time student health physician. One was the "negative reactions" and "petty jealousies" of co-workers. It is difficult for many colleagues to recognize that he pays for his three months of summer leave through reduced compensation. The second unresolved problem concerns his "inability to retain supervisory responsibilities over the long haul."

Only one other physician in the student health department followed his example. Others expressed only casual interest in part time. Dr. John Stone describes himself as "somewhat satisfied" with his current part-time situation.

Sherrill Babler
Staff Programmer, George K. Darling & Associates, North Andover, MA

As a certified public accountant and technical writer, Sherrill Babler became fascinated with computers and is pleased to be getting "state of the art" experience on a part-time basis. Ms. Babler works as a programmer for microcomputers with a small firm in Massachusetts. Earlier, she held a position as programmer and technical writer at Honeywell, a major computer manufacturer in the same state.

Work Schedule: M, W, F, 9:00 am–6:00 pm, with the option to change work days.

Fringe Benefits: Prorated vacation leave, sick leave, health insurance and profit-sharing.

Job Search Strategies: Sherrill Babler heard from a friend that Darling & Associates was seeking computer programmers. Although the firm was not in the market for part-time personnel, management accepted the idea after meeting with Ms. Babler and learning about her capabilities.

Obtaining the earlier position with Honeywell occurred in a different way. A nonprofit organization she had contacted, the Women's Work Project in Newburyport, MA, had amassed a list of individuals in various firms who were receptive to women searching for part-time employment. Sherrill Babler met with the list's "sympathetic contact" at Honeywell, who then circulated her résumé to appropriate departments within the firm. Persistence paid off when a programmer/technical writer job emerged that would use Ms. Babler's skills and accommodate her desire for reduced work hours.

Based on her successful experiences in seeking part-time professional employment, Sherrill Babler advises the following:

1. Inform the employer during your first interview that you want part-time work.

2. Build a sound network of contacts, individuals, and organizations that can help. Seek out organizations that either assist part-timers or your segment of the population—whether it be women, displaced homemakers, or retirees.

3. Do not write off any job opportunity before careful evaluation.

Solving Problems on the Job: Outsiders, especially, do not take part-timers seriously, says Sherrill Babler. Fellow employees generally respect you if you "pull your weight" at work. Others (salesmen, service people, etc.) do not get to know you and usually regard part-timers as second-rate employees. "I do not disclose my job status as a part-timer unless absolutely necessary," Ms. Babler notes. It is much easier to say, "I won't be in the office tomorrow. Can I meet with you Wednesday?" She asks the clerical support staff to respond similarly. Part time is still unusual enough, she says, that mentioning it draws attention away from business matters that have to be discussed. In a business environment, she wants attention paid to her substantive input rather than to her status as a part-time professional.

A second problem is that part-timers are less likely to work on high-visibility projects. Unfortunately the big projects usually have time requirements that do not mesh with reduced work schedules. Ms. Babler suggests that you keep your eyes open and volunteer when you can. "Sometimes all you have to do is ask." Make it a point to know what is going on, she adds. Contacts within the firm help.

The size of the firm also may be a problem for part-time professionals. In large firms, part-timers will be the first to be laid off and they may not receive benefits. But in smaller firms laying people off is harder on morale and negotiating benefits is easier to do. A part-time professional working for a larger firm must accept the fact that policies cannot be adjusted easily.

The specific strategies Sherrill Babler recommends for avoiding layoffs are:

1. Have a skill or manage an area the employer cannot afford to lose.

2. Get a mentor who will protect you.

3. If all else fails, "keep your skills up and your résumé typed. Be ready to move."

Chapter Three

Private Sector Employers

Few firms actively recruit large numbers of part-time professionals. Usually, firms start to deal with the issue of part-time work when outstanding employees ask for reduced work schedules. If the initial experience is successful, then others in the company request conversion to part time. Sometimes, the process starts with lower-level employees and then climbs the hierarchy to professionals and managers. Eventually, the employer may recognize the dollars-and-cents value of using part-time professionals and begin to open up more part-time slots to men and women outside the firm.

Turning from the experiences of other professionals who work part time, we now focus on you and your search for reduced work schedules. No national clearinghouse can point to part-time jobs in your community. There is no directory listing local employers who hire significant numbers of part-time professionals. Our advice is to start with the business firms and nonprofit organizations in your community that might be receptive to the idea of employing you as a part-time professional. Concentrate on these sympathetic prospects and avoid a random approach to targeting employers.

Like a good detective, your strategy is to identify private employers you can approach and sell on hiring you. We offer clues below as to who these employers might be. Some of these clues emerge from our study of the special characteristics of private employers that advertise to fill part-time professional vacancies, others from looking at the special characteristics of firms that are innovative and change-oriented.

Receptive Employers

The Association of Part-Time Professionals has analyzed data from 400 firms seeking to fill part-time professional positions through its job referral service in the Washington, D.C. metropolitan area. Firms that advertise for part-time professionals have six characteristics:

- Service-oriented industries. The service sector of the economy is growing, good news for part-timers since that is where most part-time jobs are. Very often, as one business reporter puts it, the service economy conjures up an image of "fast-food restaurants, dry cleaners, and bowling alleys." The reality is that the service sector accounts for seventy percent of jobs today and includes very different kinds of establishments— retail stores, wholesale distributors, telephone and power utilities, banks and insurance companies, and government. Many fast-growing service industries pay well and hire numerous professionals. These include architectural and engineering firms, legal firms, computer firms, and accounting firms.

- Traditional part-time employers. Many businesses hire large numbers of professionals in occupations that easily lend themselves to part time. So do nonprofit organizations and government agencies. Chapter One gives details on these traditional part-time professional occupations. Accountants should seek financial institutions; librarians, libraries; health professionals, hospitals and mental health centers; teachers, schools and universities; and so on.

- Small organizations. The smaller, the better. There are two main reasons for this. Managers or owners of small businesses must be especially cost-conscious. They cannot afford the luxury of "having someone around all the time" if that someone is underutilized. Personnel policies in large organizations often seem to be set in stone.

- Employers competing for scarce talent. Flexibility and accommodating employee requirements are essential for these firms. Engineering firms, computer organizations, and health-care facilities top the list here. Do not ignore other firms, nonprofit organizations, and government agencies that also need professionals with scarce skills. Employers will take you, full time or part time, if you have hard–to–find capabilities.

- Women in management. Women are more likely to sympathize with the desire to work part time. Personal experience plus the testimony of friends and business colleagues prove to them the advantages of part-time work for both workers and employers. As women move into positions of authority, they are beginning to press for changes in personnel policy. You should be aware, however, that another attitude also prevails among a minority of female executives. These women have worked long hours, full time, making career advancement their number-one priority. Their philosophy regarding female professionals desiring to work part time is: "I did it and managed. Why can't you?"

- Nonunion employers. Unions generally oppose part-time, although there is evidence that union attitudes are changing. For unions, exploitation of part-time workers is the issue—they oppose employers hiring part-timers at lower wages, without fringe benefits, and taking jobs away from full-time employees. While most professional jobs are not unionized, strong unions at other levels may inhibit management's flexibility even for workers not covered by bargaining agreements.

The Conference Board in New York (a nonprofit business-research organization) is studying corporate programs that help to alleviate conflicts between work and family. Alternative work patterns, including part time, are among the corporate practices under review. Helen Axel of the Board's Work and Family Information Center concurs that firms with large numbers of women and companies that are largely or entirely nonunion are more receptive to new personnel policies. She identifies the following special characteristics of firms receptive to innovation and change:

- Firms employing a relatively young work force. Because these firms usually have employees with family responsibilities, they tend to be more flexible.

- High-technology, high-growth firms. These companies have to compete for employees and must be accommodating.

- Consumer-oriented businesses. Here, the firm identifies the employee as a customer and may be more responsive to the employee customer population.

- Companies with "social conscience." These are firms active in the community that want to mirror their good works within the corporation.

Exercise 2:

Identify ten firms in your community which (a) are described by one or more of the special characteristics noted above, *and* (b) use your professional skills.

Sources of information for finding these receptive firms are found in Chapter Six, page 68. Fill in below the names, addresses, and phone numbers of these prospective employers.

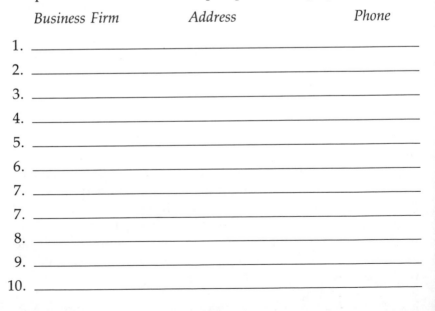

	Business Firm	*Address*	*Phone*
1.			
2.			
3.			
4.			
5.			
6.			
7.			
7.			
8.			
9.			
10.			

Firms Using Part-Time Professionals

Across the country, businesses with one or more of the above special characteristics are using part-time professionals. We want you to be aware of some of these companies. Then, when you are talking to the managers of an insurance company, for example, you can mention other insurance firms that successfully use part-timers. Knowing about specific examples also builds confidence among prospective part-time professionals that like-minded firms exist in their communities.

Merck & Co., Inc.

Merck & Co., a leading pharmaceutical firm, recognizes that the American work force is changing and that corporate practices must adapt to take advantage of these changes. In response, Merck & Co. has introduced several significant innovations:

- Flexi–time is in place at most of Merck's domestic operations.

- Merck has provided financial assistance and initial direction in establishing two child-care centers in New Jersey and Pennsylvania.

- The company has spearheaded formation of a consortium of companies in northern New Jersey to provide assistance in locating employment opportunities for working spouses of newly hired and relocated employees.

- Merck has undertaken an on-going study of alternate work patterns, including permanent part time, phased retirement, job sharing, flexi–place, and other nontraditional approaches.

A number of permanent part-time opportunities are opening up at Merck, although part time still is in a testing situation. So far, employees are using part time mainly for child-care purposes. About twenty-five to thirty women and about ten men have opted for some version of part-time employment over the past three years. Occupationally diverse, the part-timers are managers, professionals, and clerical staff. Because of the part-time option, female workers often return earlier following maternity leave.

Merck also recruits some part-time professionals from outside the firm. In the labs, for example, there may be extra work that needs to be done, but does not warrant a full-time person.

Rationale for Innovations

Why did Merck & Co. introduce innovations which, a few years ago, would not have been considered a corporate responsibility? Why does the company foresee accelerating action on work place and work time flexibility? Art Strohmer, executive director of human resource planning and development, suggests some reasons:

- Merck's own work force is dramatically different today. The company sees a diversity of lifestyles, more dual-career couples, and increasing numbers of working women and working mothers. These demographic changes, at Merck and throughout America, have produced the potential for increased conflict between work and family life.

- The company's desire for improved productivity requires company action to minimize the potential stresses between work and personal life.

- Merck's employees want more flexible time schedules, more support for family-related needs, and reasonable adjustment of work procedures to better meet individual needs. The challenge for Merck and other companies, says Mr. Strohmer, is to respond to employees' needs in ways that will not negatively affect productivity—ways that might even enhance productivity.

Resistance to Innovation

Merck also recognizes that many managers have grown up with traditional work values and work patterns. These managers often see no need to change. Art Strohmer has found that there is some resistance to an increased corporate role in providing programs that support lifestyle changes and changes in family structure. On occasion, deeply-ingrained traditional beliefs must be overcome:

- The belief that an individual's life situation is his/her own personal responsibility—completely separate from the corporation.

- The belief that it is *not* the role of the corporation to solve—or become heavily involved in—what is essentially a "non-work" arena.

- The belief, and fear, that many work place innovations will negatively affect productivity and dilute the control managers have over their employees.

Workplace changes must occur if companies are to perform successfully, but the resistance to change means that innovations will be introduced slowly, cautiously, and only after considerable testing. The danger to companies and employees is that the response will be too little and too late.

The Orkand Corporation

The Orkand Corporation was founded in 1970 by Dr. Donald S. Orkand with the basic commitment to provide information systems and analysis services of highest quality for government, business, and industry clients.

Part-time professionals comprise approximately ten percent of the total workforce of over 300 staff members. Specifically, The Orkand Corporation hires programmers, systems analysts, technical writers, and other degreed individuals. The firm also employs another ten percent of nonprofessional personnel (clerks, typists, data entry, etc.).

Historically, The Orkand Corporation did not hire part-time staff. However, as the competition for qualified information systems professionals in the Washington, D.C. area increased, The Orkand Corporation decided to tap the group of talented professionals who preferred to work on a part-time basis. Kathleen McCasland, manager of recruiting, commented that the part-time employees had excellent technical skills and as a whole "were some of our most conscientious and dependable employees." She added, "The initial problem with hiring part-time employees was learning to integrate them successfully into the demanding schedules of our projects. However, our managers are now accustomed to this."

Benefits for part-time employees are rolled into their salaries. The Orkand Corporation uses a formula which includes compensation for holidays, health insurance, and vacation time that is added on to the part-time employee's hourly rate.

Control Data Corporation

A large computer-products and information-services firm based in Minneapolis, Control Data Corporation employs part-time workers throughout its operations. Part-timers (called "supplementals") work 32 hours or less per week and earn a separate benefits package by working 900 hours or more in the preceding year. Although the majority of Control Data's part-time jobs are clerical and production, the part-time option is available in professional areas.

Part-time professionals comprise about ten percent of Control Data's supplemental contingent. Administrators occupy about one-half of these slots with the remainder divided evenly among managers, sales personnel, programmers, and engineers. Most part-time professionals are women seeking flexible work settings to meet their changing needs, says Patrick Vincelli, manager of corporate staffing services.

Flexibility in work scheduling and the high morale of part-timers are two advantages of the part-time option for Control Data. Employee expectations can be a problem, however, since some part-timers hire on as supplementals looking for full-time work. Building a "buffer work force" to increase job security for full-time employees is another major reason for Control Data's interest in part-time work. Currently, the policies and practices related to this buffer work force are being studied and evaluated.

Viewed as a management tool and not a social service program, the use of part-time professionals is expanding at Control Data. Mr. Vincelli notes that "part time meets both the employee's needs and ours." He suggests that professionals contact the Control Data personnel offices in their areas to see if there are openings to match their skills.

Coopers & Lybrand

Part-time professional employment is becoming more prevalent among professional services firms, says Sal Luiso, assistant to the chairman of Coopers & Lybrand, a public accounting firm with headquarters in New York City. The major reason: more women are entering nontraditional employment areas, are doing well, and then are deciding they want to start families. Other part-timers are retirees wishing to continue working, but on a reduced schedule and employees choosing to return to school for advanced degrees.

Accountants and tax professionals are the key part-time professional positions filled at Coopers & Lybrand. Part-time work developed at the professional level because initial arrangements succeeded and then spread among the firm's ninety-five offices around the country. Coopers & Lybrand employs professionals on different part-time schedules: full-time, part-time schedules (full-time, part of the year) and permanent part-time (permanent and part-time all of the year). Part-time professionals receive a "core" benefits package.

Mr. Luiso states that "part-time work evolved as a way of doing business rather than as a result of a policy declared in writing. It made sense. It is good business." "Part-time arrangements," Mr. Luiso concludes, "are mutually beneficial. They fill a need. Accommodation is not the term to describe them. Part-time work is not something management is doing for professionals. It is management working with people."

Ameritrust Corporation

Getting the best available people, says employment specialist Lois Goodman of Ameritrust in Cleveland, Ohio, is the motivation for using professionals on part-time schedules. It is "wise recruiting," she notes, and taps an excellent work force that is underutilized because these professionals will only work part time.

The firm currently employs twenty part-time professionals. They occupy a wide range of jobs, including an attorney, a trust officer, a compensation and benefits specialist, and a computer programmer. Part-timers receive a full range of benefits on a prorated basis.

Ameritrust hires from the outside to fill part-time vacancies and also works with current full-time employees who wish to reduce their work schedules. Favorable experiences with part–time workers at the clerical level helped bring the option into the professional ranks. The fact that the company did not have to invent a compensation and benefit structure for professionals also was a plus.

The only disadvantage, Ms. Goodman admits, is for the workers. Managerial responsibilities cannot be assumed by part-timers. "The upside," she adds, "is that professional workers can continue uninterrupted career growth and development while maintaining a part-time schedule. If and when their schedules change to full-time employment, they are ready and prepared to assume managerial jobs."

The Travelers Insurance Companies

A keen sense of social responsibility and the need to cut personnel costs led to the development of Travelers' highly acclaimed program of rehiring the firm's own retirees on reduced-work schedules. Retirees can work up to 900 hours per year—as temporary employees, as permanent part-timers, or as job sharers—and still receive pensions. The rehired annuitants are, to use a popular phrase, "double dippers."

The program is so successful that management always votes to continue it, says Georgina Lucas, administrator of the Travelers Older Americans Program. The retirees are familiar with the company and the work, and they require little orientation or training. Cost savings are considerable.

Some problems do occur. Holidays and peak vacation times are difficult to cover. Some retirees are unfamiliar with automated equipment and are intimidated by it. Finally, the supply of retirees cannot meet the demand.

Evelyn Smith and Sylvia Corvo, co-directors of the firm's retiree job bank, report that many professionals are placed through the service. Officers on special projects, chief underwriters, position classification specialists, and proofreaders are examples. In 1983, the job bank processed 404 jobs; the 1984 totals are higher.

Kaiser Foundation Health Plan, Inc. (Kaiser Permanente)

Health care facilities—hospitals, medical centers, clinics—are well-known users of part-timers at all skill levels. Part-time employees extend hours of service, provide expert services not needed full time, and reduce the incidence of burnout in high-stress occupations.

Kaiser Permanente, the nation's largest health-maintenance organization with headquarters in Oakland, California, uses part-timers extensively. Gretchen Seifert, vice president for quality assurance, points to one Kaiser hospital on the West Coast as an example. It employs 400 part-timers out of 1,200 full-time equivalent employees. Individuals working 20 hours or more per week receive full benefits, prorated.

From an operations standpoint, Ms. Seifert remarks, part-time people are very flexible. They work difficult hours, yet the reduced schedules permit employees to continue with their particular lifestyles. Many nurses, for example, rely on part-time hours to attend school. The negative factor, she adds, is lack of continuity on the job.

Many part-time professional positions exist in Kaiser facilities, including nurses, physicians, physical therapists, lab technicians, and psychologists. Many hospitals also employ part-time dietitians and social workers. Kaiser first posts part-time vacancies internally and then recruits from the outside. Administrators try to avoid conversions from full-time to part-time status. This structured program of recruiting for part-time positions eliminates any suspicion of favoritism.

Northern Natural Gas Co.

"Employing part-time professionals is part of our company's adjustment to changing times and conditions," says John Anderson, director of employee relations services at Northern Natural Gas in Omaha. In our industry, there is "quite a bit of reorganization." We are "using people differently" and are interested in more "economic and efficient" ways of doing things.

Many female professionals who have built up areas of skill and expertise valuable to the company are returning from maternity leave and want to continue their careers on a regular part-time basis. On several occasions, these women have been able to come back to the same or to higher-level professional positions on a part-time basis. Eventually, many revert to full-time status.

The part-time solution for professionals has worked out very well, according to Mr. Anderson. There is no formal plan for this; it has resulted from opportunities presenting themselves. In the past year, he notes, four or five people converted to part-time schedules.

Nonprofit Organizations

Do not ignore nonprofit organizations in your search for receptive employers. Nonprofits include social service agencies, public policy organizations, professional societies, trade associations, health-care agencies, educational facilities, and community-based organizations. Our recommendation is to explore carefully the personnel needs of your local nonprofit organizations.

Today these nonprofits are stretched for funds as they struggle to serve members and the public with reduced staff. Target selected nonprofit organizations and show how you, as a part-time professional, can help them achieve their service goals at a lower cost. Dr. Monique Cohen explains how she did it in Chapter Six.

Exercise 3:

Identify three nonprofit organizations in your community which use your professional skills. Sources of information for finding these organizations are found in Chapter Six, page 68.

Fill in below the names, addresses, and phone numbers of these prospective employers.

Nonprofit Organization	Address	Phone

1. _____

2. _____

3. _____

Employer Motivation

Business firms competing for scarce talents probably are the private sector employers most willing to accommodate part-time professionals. Often, they are high-tech, high-growth firms that also may have a relatively young work force. Note the experience of Sherrill Babler in Chapter Two and Dean Lauver in Chapter Six in transforming scarce professional skills into part-time jobs. In other cases, traditional service industries, such as banks and insurance companies, require large numbers of personnel with scarce skills. Sometimes, high-tech firms are heavily involved in government contract work and are required to establish affirmative action goals for women and minorities. Hiring part-time professionals is a natural for them.

Retaining key professionals who are experienced and top performers is a high priority for most companies. Very often, this is an opening wedge for professionals in the company to ask for conversion to part-time hours. Flexibility is a must for companies that recognize that these employees can quit and find work with competitors. Some firms, large and small, use sizeable numbers of part-time professionals because their businesses demand it. They include research firms or companies with significant research programs, publishers, and health care organizations. Barbara Kelley's experiences as a librarian (Chapter Two) and Anne Reid's as an editor (Chapter Five) are examples of these kinds of careers.

Financial services firms are acknowledged employers of part-timers. Often, these firms have opened up large numbers of clerical positions to part-timers—their own retirees or outsiders. As part-time work becomes established at lower skill levels, they may become receptive to professionals inside the organization desiring to convert to part time.

The bottom line for most profit-making enterprises using part-time professionals is that it pays. It is good business. It solves a real problem or meets a real need. It is in the best interest of the company and the employee.

Chapter Four

Selling the Employer

Initiative, perseverance, and skill are essential to become a part-time professional. As you prepare your employer-targeting plan, recognize you must overcome some hostility, even among the types of employers we have identified as receptive to requests for shorter work schedules.

Understand these employers' attitudes. Often, employers equate the serious, dedicated professional with the individual who works long hours. Working a reduced week is the equivalent of unprofessional conduct in the minds of employers. U.S. Representative Pat Schroeder calls these attitudes a "negative mind set." Dr. Stanley Nollen of Georgetown University labels them "cultural stereotypes." Whatever the term, prospective part-time professionals must be aware of these negatives.

Lack of interest by employers also is a problem. A realistic explanation for this absence of concern comes from Dr. Nollen:

> "For most employers, part-time employment is simply not an issue. . . . It is not sufficiently important in the whole context of running the business that it deserves or warrants any special attention on its own. You see, work schedules, of which part-time employment is only one, are only a part of human resource management, and that is only part of the making and selling of a product."

Many employers do not realize that highly competent men and women desire part-time employment. Do not underestimate the employer's lack of knowledge on this subject. Repeatedly, managers assert that professionals do not want to work part time. Employers believe this because few professionals ask for reduced work schedules.

Overcoming employer resistance requires skilled marketing by you, the prospective part-time professional. You must demonstrate concretely and persuasively the advantages to management of employing you as a part-time professional.

Advantages to Management

It is hard to get any manager to try something new, particularly if the old way seems to be operating reasonably well. You must know, and confidently talk about, what can be achieved by changing established work patterns. Emphasize to the employer why part time will work for the organization, *not* why you want to work part time. The advantages to the employer will far outweigh any difficulties in implementing an innovative work arrangement.

Picture yourself as a manager trying to get the job done as efficiently as possible. You are trying to hold down costs and increase productivity in the competitive world of the 1980's.

Exercise 4:

Write down the reasons why a manager should hire you as a part-time professional. Check your answers against the advantages discussed below.

1. _____

_____

2. _____

_____

3. _____

_____

4. _____

_____

5. _____

_____

6. _____

_____

Emphasize those of the following advantages that apply to the specific employer you are targeting. Downplay the personal benefits to you or the general benefits to society of part-time professional employment. Concentrate on the employer's self-interest.

- Increased productivity. Most part-timers testify they waste less time on the job than they did in a full-time capacity. When they are on the job, they are working. They also are aware that good part-time professional jobs are harder to find than full-time jobs, so they are eager to perform well. Part-time professionals are motivated workers who are less affected by fatigue and stress.

- Reduced absenteeism and turnover. Studies show that part-time professionals take less time off from work. Personal obligations are taken care of on their time, not the employer's. Also, part-time professionals stay on the job longer, again because good part-time jobs are hard to find.

- Valuable employees retained. Skills and experience are not lost to the employer because current full-time personnel, especially women with children and older workers facing retirement, do not have to make that "all or nothing" decision about working. Employers can eliminate some training costs and maintain continuity in work to be done by retaining these employees.

- More precise matching of skills to tasks. Qualified part-timers can be hired for whatever time a job requires. It is not necessary to fill up an employee's week or to assign tasks which could be more efficiently handled by another.

- Scarce talent recruited. Critical job shortages can be filled by establishing part-time professional positions. There is a pool of scarce professional talent waiting to be tapped by employers willing to satisfy workers' needs for reduced hours.

- Greater flexibility in work schedules. Part-time professionals can increase their work hours in crisis periods, can be employed during peak hours of business, can be assigned specific projects to complete, and can extend the employer's hours of service.

- <u>Upgrading skills.</u> The option of working part time enables current employees to improve their professional skills through continuing education.

- <u>Reduced burnout.</u> Many professionals leave jobs after years of stress and fatigue. Reduced working hours can provide needed time to recharge energy and motivation.

- <u>Better employer–employee relations.</u> Flexibility and the willingness to be innovative demonstrate a concerned employer. Satisfied professionals are better workers than those who resent rigid personnel policies.

Answering Objections to Part Time

Employing part-time professionals may be a new idea for your prospective employer. Understandably, the employer will raise many questions about how the proposed schedule will work and its impact on the rest of the company. Be prepared to handle the employer's questions and objections in a confident, informed manner.

Exercise 5:

(a) Pretend you are an employer. List below the objections you, *as an employer*, may have to professionals working part time.

(b) Then, pretend you are a prospective part-time professional. Answer each objection raised by the employer and provide a counterargument.

Check your answers against the objections and counterarguments discussed in the text following Exercise 5.

Objection 1. _____

_____

Counterargument 1. _____

_____

Objection 2. _____

_____

Counterargument 2. _____

_____

Objection 3. _____

_____

Counterargument 3. _____

_____

Objection 4. _____

_____

Counterargument 4. _____

_____

- "Employing part-time professionals means more costly fringe benefits for my company, does it not?"

  Turn to Chapter Seven for a full discussion of employee benefits as applied to part-timers. It is important to understand these facts. Employers pay very modest additional costs when they hire part-time professionals. Almost all benefits can be prorated.

- "How can you be serious about your profession and want to work part time?"

  Concern about handling both professional and personal responsibilities well leads you to prefer part-time work. You know you can do a better job as a part-timer. The Association of Part-Time Professionals has hundreds of serious, committed members across the country to back up this claim.

- "What happens when you are not here and someone needs you?"

  Full-time workers do not sit at their desks eight hours a day, five days a week. Messages are taken for them and they schedule appointments in advance; they also arrange to be present for important meetings. Part-time professionals do the same and, when necessary, can be reached by phone at home during "off-duty" hours. Continuity in work can be maintained with advance planning.

- "How will you know what goes on during your absence?"

  Part-time professionals accept the responsibility for setting up an effective communication system to stay informed. Full-time people face the same challenge when on vacation, business trips, or out of the office for large portions of the day. Communications between part-time and full-time personnel are not a major problem in organizations that value good communication.

- "Co-workers will resent you; you cannot prevent that, can you?"

  There will be less resentment if full-time employees are informed about the new working arrangements and reminded that part-time professionals take home part-time paychecks.

- "I'll have higher record-keeping costs."

  Record-keeping costs are negligible unless there is a large part-time work force. These costs can be minimized by a personnel system that prorates salaries and benefits for part-time professionals. Computerized record-keeping speeds up this process.

- "What about the time involved in training and supervising more employees?"

  Some training costs may actually be saved by retaining full-time employees. Since there are fewer part-time professional positions available compared to demand, more qualified candidates usually apply. Recruiting costs go down as turnover and absenteeism decrease. Supervisory costs should be minimal because any one section or department would not employ large numbers of part-time professionals. In any case, supervision should not entail constant oversight of professional employees.

- "If I start with you, everyone will want to work part time."

  A survey of employees would answer this question. Not everyone wants to, or can, work less than full time. Many more people indicate an interest in part time than are ready to accept reduced pay.

- "Part time may work for clericals, but not for supervisors and managers."

  Effective managers can be part time, depending on the programs they are supervising and the skills of their employees. A part-time arrangement is appropriate where higher-skilled employees are being supervised, where creative management is important, or where there is real danger of managerial "burnout." Managerial tasks should not preclude automatically part-time status. Check Chapters One and Two for examples of managers that work part time.

- "Will I have to secure new desks and equipment for these extra people?"

  Scheduling part-timers at alternate times can avoid logistical problems.

- "Our firm has never done this before."

Suggest a trial period of three months to see how the part-time innovation works out. Also, cite examples of companies in the same industry who do employ part-time professionals. Recognize that a prospective employer who has never tried part-time professionals may not verbalize all his/her reservations about reduced hours of work. Silent questions may be on the employer's mind. For example, "If I start using part-time professionals, will it look as though my department can make do with fewer people and money?" The answer always is to show how part time serves the employer's own interest and how the employer will benefit from using your services.

Anticipating an employer's questions and objections is smart behavior whether you are in an interview situation or are developing a proposal for a part-time professional position. Stress the advantages of employing you as a part-time professional and counter the myths and misconceptions that surround this subject.

Chapter Five

Converting Your Full-Time Job to Part Time

Converting your full-time job to part time is an outstanding option whether you work for a busness firm or in a government agency. As a current full-time employee, you understand your job and your organization's operations. Since you are a valued employee your boss does not want to lose, you have an advantage in presenting the case for part-time employment. Note the examples of Elaine Walter and Dr. John Stone in Chapter Two and the success stories of Lynne Heltman and Anne Reid at the end of this chapter.

Very often, a private employer confronts the issue of part-time employment at the professional level for the first time when an experienced employee desires to cut back hours. If the employee presents a persuasive case, management tends to be responsive. Reflect for a moment and you will understand why a full-time professional seeking conversion to part time is in a strong position:

- The cost to an employer of recruiting and training a replacement will be high.
- Continuity in tasks and relationships will be maintained if the employee's reduced work schedule can be accommodated.
- A skilled employee with proven capabilities will be retained.

- Flexibility shows that the employer cares about staff members—a boost to employee morale.

- Restructuring one person's job can be the impetus for management to review the entire operation of an office or program. Improved performance can result.

Your First Step

Review your organization's official personnel policies. Most likely, there will be no prohibitions against part-time employment at professional levels. Neither will there be formal policies encouraging part-time employment. Find out if your organization's rules and regulations make exceptions for special groups—married women with children, or older workers nearing retirement. More flexibility in work hours and conditions may be allowed for these special groups. Investigate precisely how these special policies have been applied in the past. Personnel practices often differ from the formal rules. A key to actual practice is whether any professionals in your organization already work part time.

Track down the part-time professionals inside your firm. Obtain detailed information about the specific circumstances of their part-time assignments. Get their advice and support. The more part-timers you talk with, the more you will understand your organization's internal dynamics. Learn how and why professionals in your organization succeeded in obtaining their part-time positions:

- Who approved their part-time slots? Did approval involve only an immediate supervisor? Was top management involved? What was the personnel department's role? Make it your business to get to know the people involved in employment practices.

- Do the jobs of current part-time professionals have special characteristics? Are scarce job skills involved? Are these jobs with peak workloads or high stress? Do the part-timers work on relatively independent projects?

Learning about current part-time professional jobs will provide clues to what is already acceptable practice in your organization. Your fact–finding will help you avoid personal and organizational roadblocks on your way to part-time status.

Looking at Your Job

Your current full-time job must be thoroughly analyzed since you want to convert this position to part time. Keep a log for two months showing tasks performed on the job. Do not be fancy; a small notebook will do. Analyze your daily routine and be precise about your activities—telephoned client, wrote memo, attended staff meeting, researched a case.

Exercise 6:

Start your daily log immediately. After two months you will have forty to forty-five pages of daily activities, each page looking like the following chart, with the blanks filled in.

Daily Activities

Day:_____ Month:_____

	Activity 1	Activity 2	Activity 3	Activity 4	Activity 5
9:00-10:00 am					
10:00-11:00					
11:00-12 noon					
12:00-1:00 pm					
1:00-2:00					
2:00-3:00					
3:00-4:00					
4:00-5:00					

These activities are the tasks that comprise your job. Tasks you enjoy should comprise the core of your proposed part-time job. Excess components of the job can be done by another worker, possibly someone less highly paid.

Negotiating with Your Employer

If you merely present a nebulous suggestion about cutting back your hours, you risk antagonizing your boss because the effort needed to accommodate you may not seem worthwhile. Offering a concrete, carefully documented proposal enhances your credibility and the chances for your proposal's adoption.

You will have to decide which person to approach with your proposal—your immediate supervisor or a manager further up the line. Our advice is to approach your immediate boss first because you want that individual on your side. Although final authority may rest in other hands, it is valuable for higher-level managers to know that your own boss supports your request. Remember, as your first step in the conversion process, you found out who has authority to approve part-time slots. As you draw up your proposal, make sure to:

- Determine the best way to approach your supervisor. Should you present your proposal in writing or orally? Do you make an appointment to present your request, or do you watch for a chance encounter to discuss the issue? If you decide on an appointment, should it be for lunch or in regular office surroundings? You are the best judge in answering these questions. Presumably you have built up a good working relationship with your employer and you know how best to communicate with that individual.

- Show precisely what job tasks you will continue to perform on a part-time basis. Recommend ways other people can take over part of the workload.

- Give examples, if you can, of your organization's use of part-time professionals. Managers, even innovative ones, prefer to adopt already tested practices. It will help your case if you can document successful use of part-timers inside your organization.

- Stress the advantages to your employer of having you as a part-timer. Present yourself as a valuable asset. You are there and know the job and organization very well. It will take time and money to train someone to replace you. If applicable, show how your nonwork pursuits directly or indirectly assist your employer.

- Be prepared to answer your employer's questions and to defend the proposal.

- Suggest a trial period of three to six months. Experience shows that a trial run often convinces managers about the feasibility of part time.

- Decide ahead of time whether or not you will resign if your request is denied. Do not make a rash decision if you are disappointed. Do not threaten to quit unless you mean it. Specific guidance comes from part-time professionals who successfully converted from full time:

  "I informed my chief that I would quit if I could not get a part-time position. If they are pleased with your work, most will bend if they can."

  "Don't waiver in your position. Let them think they may lose you even though you know you need the job."

  "Make it clear you are seeking part-time work in your current organization or another."

In short, be firm in your commitment to part time. Be pleasant but negotiate hard.

Although your immediate boss may not be open to the part-time alternative, a manager in another department may be. Your initial investigation should have pinpointed other likely spots for part-time professionals. Do not hesitate to approach these managers if your boss denies your request for reduced hours.

Exercise 7:

Define the issues you must face in developing a proposal to convert your present job to part time. Provide the answers in the worksheet below.

1. Your approach to your supervisor_____

_____

_____

2. Your job responsibilities and tasks as a part-time professional

_____

_____

_____

3. Your organization's present use of part-time professionals

_____

_____

4. Advantages to your employer of your conversion to part time

_____

_____

_____

_____

_____

5. Your employer's possible questions and objections_____

_____

_____

_____

_____

_____

6. How a trial period might work_____

_____

_____

_____

7. If your employer refuses your request for conversion to part time_____

_____

_____

_____

_____

Success Stories

Successfully converting your full-time professional job to part time requires great sensitivity to your organization's requirements and to the personalities involved. Also, you have to be recognized as a top producer. Here are some ideas from two part-time professionals who succeeded. Consult Chapters One and Two for additional examples of professionals working full time who converted to part time.

Lynne Heltman
Statistician, Veterans Administration, Washington, D.C.

Prior to her part-time position with the Veterans Administration, Lynne Heltman worked as a civil rights analyst for the U.S. Commission on Civil Rights. After returning from maternity leave she wanted to cut back her full-time workload, but the staff director—a woman—strongly resisted the idea. Ms. Heltman appealed to the staff director's supervisor and was given permission to try the part-time option for six months. This temporary part-time assignment became permanent after two years.

Persistence paid off for Lynne Heltman at the Civil Rights Commission. She consistently stated her intention to resign if the part-time option was not available. A year later, she took a second maternity leave, returning to work twenty hours weekly. Within a year she resigned from her job. Her workload was heavier, she believed, than her part-time hours warranted, and her performance evaluation report did not take this fact into account.

Shortly after resigning, she applied for two full-time positions—one at the U.S. Department of Education and a second at the Veterans Administration. At the end of each interview, only after establishing mutual interest, she mentioned the fact that she required a part-time position.

"What I thought should concern the employers most," she says, "was not that I needed part-time hours. It was my experience and capabilities." For that reason, she discussed her requirements for part-time hours only toward the end of each interview.

Operating in her favor at both federal agencies was their positive experiences with the performance of other part-timers. The part-time precedent had been established before Lynne Heltman appeared on the scene. As one manager expressed it: "The part-timers accomplish as much as the full-time people." At the Department of Education, she spoke with a part-time professional there as part of the interview. Although both agencies made her job offers, she signed on with the Veterans Administration. Ms. Heltman works four days a week as a statistician, providing estimates and projections of the veteran population. In late 1984, she requested a two-hour reduction in her work week in order to pick up her daughter at school. The request won easy approval.

Anne Reid
Editor, Houghton Mifflin Co., Boston, MA

As an editor with a major publishing house, Anne Reid reads and edits college science textbook manuscripts and works with authors to make sure the manuscripts are well written, with competitive coverage of topics and proper level of presentation.

After working for the company for ten years, she arranged for a three-day work week after maternity leave, giving up a job that included managerial and supervisory duties. She recommends the following strategies for converting from full-time to part-time work:

- Become a known and valued quantity in a full-time job beforehand.

- Work out a part-time position well in advance of the date you wish to start. Be prepared to think through and lead discussion of all issues involved since other people have different priorities and no real reason to go out on a limb for you.

- Work through your own boss and management and avoid ultimatums, but be as informed as possible by networking with other part-timers and by keeping in touch (cautiously) with the personnel department.

Chapter Six

Obtaining A Part-Time Professional Job as an Outsider

As an outsider, there are three ways you can start work as a part-time professional:

1. You respond to an existing, advertised opening for a part-time professional job and are hired to fill the vacancy.

2. You learn about a vacancy for a full-time professional job, and you convince the hiring official that this job can be performed by you part time.

3. You create your own part-time professional position by persuading a prospective employer that you have something special to offer.

As an outsider, you also must recognize that it is more difficult to persuade an employer to hire you on a part-time arrangement. Basically, your employer–targeting strategy is either find an existing vacancy or shop around for a receptive employer.

Take seriously the information already presented in Chapter Three on private sector employers and look carefully at Chapters Nine and Ten on government agencies. Note particularly the "special characteristics" of employers we suggest will more likely hire you from the outside as a part-time professional:

- Service-oriented industries
- Traditional part-time employers
- Small organizations
- Employers competing for scarce talent
- Women in management
- Nonunion employers
- Young work force
- High-technology, high-growth firms
- Consumer–oriented businesses
- Socially conscious firms that are active in the community

Sources of Information

Multiple job-hunting resources are available to you in your community. Review the following list of potential leads carefully and take time to do the suggested exercise:

- Your personal network. This is your most important source of information about existing or possible vacancies. Friends, relatives, former employers, and colleagues in past or present jobs see job openings at their own firms or government agencies. Tell everyone you know that you are job hunting. Networking is successful even in government. Have friends invite you to business meetings and luncheons to build contacts.

- Newspapers. Newspapers list part-time professional jobs, but the listings are well hidden. Generally, these jobs do not appear under the heading "part time." Instead, they will be under the occupational head and you may have to read carefully to see the term "part time" or the number of hours specified. Sometimes, employers will use the term "contract employees." This is a hint they may be flexible about work schedules.

- Professional associations. Almost all professional associations maintain information on members seeking jobs and on available positions. Sometimes, vacancies are announced in chapter newsletters. Other associations may run job banks which either notify you of openings or forward your résumé to interested employers. There may be a fee for this service.

- Universities. Most universities operate some type of job clearinghouse for current students and graduates. Many part-time jobs listed through the clearinghouses are professional. Some offices mail out job bulletins. At others, you go to the office to check listings. You do not always need to be a graduate of the institution to gain access to these job services. Another approach is to seek out faculty members teaching business and public administration. Faculty members often are used as resources by employers in the market for professional help. Do not ignore this important source of information.

- Career counseling centers. Many nonprofit career counseling centers exist throughout the country. Usually subsidized by local governments, they may be oriented toward a specific group—re-entry women, for example, or senior citizens. These counseling centers maintain job banks as part of their services.

- Organizational networks. Numerous organizations exist whose purpose is to foster business contacts. Some examples are Business and Professional Women's Clubs and Forty Plus. While much of their networking is informal, many organizations publish job leads in local newsletters. The Washington Area Chapter of the Association of Part-Time Professionals (APTP) operates a job referral service and publishes a newsletter with local job listings. Other APTP networks in your area may have information on local jobs. Professionals also meet in service clubs, political groups, and alumnae organizations. An important by–product of these interactions is networking for job leads.

- Libraries. Many libraries have an area set aside to help job hunters. Books, newsletters, and pamphlets on jobs often are available there. The business section, with references to local businesses, also is a valuable resource.

Exercise 8:

List the information sources in your community that can aid you in job hunting. Be specific. Use additional worksheets as needed.

	Name	Address	Phone

Your personal network
   friends
   relatives
   former employers
   colleagues
   others

Newspapers

Professional associations

Universities
   job clearinghouses
   job bulletins
   professors

Career counseling centers

Organization networks

Libraries

Advertised Vacancies

An estimated twenty percent of full-time jobs are advertised publicly. This is probably true for part-time jobs also. Our advice is pay attention to the advertised jobs. Of course, do not stop there. Penetrate the "hidden" job market, but be sure you do not neglect advertised part-time professional positions.

Make sure you are plugged into all the networks where you can hear and read about existing part-time vacancies. Actual openings are circulated by word-of-mouth or in written announcements. Be a joiner. Keep meeting and talking to people with interests similar to yours.

Informational interviews, if you can obtain them, are very valuable. Personnel officials and operating managers sometimes will take the time to talk with professionals who seek their advice on job-related matters. Do not use an informational interview to ask for a specific job. Discuss, as a serious professional, the potential for part-time employment in that industry. As a bonus, you may obtain leads about possible part-time openings in your field.

Using Full-Time Vacancies as Leads

As you progress in your job-search activities, you may learn that a full-time vacancy exists in your field. Our advice is to apply for this opening.

Send a cover letter and résumé demonstrating your accomplishments and qualifications for the position. Some part-time professionals, especially those in high-demand occupations, specify in cover letters and telephone calls to employers that they are looking only for part-time work. Since the purpose of the cover letter and résumé is to secure an interview, we recommend that you *do not* indicate that you wish to work part time. You will explore the part-time option during the interview.

As Chapter Eight on learning to negotiate explains, you avoid starting with "specifics" in an initial interview. Hours of employment are a "specific." The main purpose of the initial interview is exchanging information about job responsibilities and applicant skills. Discussing a part-time schedule first is inappropriate. Highlighting your desire for part-time work in a cover letter or résumé is similarly inappropriate.

Let us say that, happily, your cover letter and résumé impressed the recruiting official. You are called in for an interview. Immediately look for specific information about the organization and the full-time vacancy. You want as many details as possible prior to the interview so you can demonstrate convincingly how the entire job, or a substantial portion of the tasks, can be performed part time.

Be realistic about how much a job can be cut back. An employer who has advertised a full-time position is unlikely to reduce it below thirty hours per week. If you are unable to work this much, investigate the advantages of splitting the job into two part-time positions or consider job sharing. Research your targeted employer for the following:

- The firm's official personnel policies. Do official policies discuss part time? Are there special rules and regulations for particular groups, for example, married women with children or older workers? Then go beyond formal policies to informal practices.

- Part-time professionals already employed by the firm. Who hired them? What are the special characteristics of their jobs? Have problems surfaced about part-time schedules? Talk to these part-time professionals to understand the way the firm really operates.

During the interview, you hit it off very well with the interviewer. Gradually, the discussion turns to specifics about the job—salary, hours of work, career paths. You may be asked to return for a further meeting with others who will make the hiring decision. At this point, when the employer starts talking about job specifics, open up the subject of flexible hours. Mention a reduced work schedule. Emphasize the advantages to the employer of hiring you as a part-time professional. Orally, during the interview, or in a written proposal following the interview:

- Show specifically how the entire job can be done in fewer hours. Offer this option only if you believe it is realistic and feasible. An alternative is to detail which job tasks can be performed by you part time. Show how others can accomplish the residual tasks which you cannot perform on a reduced schedule.

- Offer to the employer your own version of flexitime. Suggest a minimum number of hours each week that you will work. This gives you a base salary, and your employer knows you can be counted on for at least these hours. Establish a range of hours above the base when you can work and be reimbursed. When the workload is down, you will be much less expensive to carry on the payroll than a full-time employee. When work is heavy, the employer knows she/he can rely on you for extra hours.

- Suggest a trial period. Many employers are reluctant to admit, unless shown, that the work can be done outside the sacred forty to fifty hour week. Note your willingness to forego employee benefits until the trial period is over. Many private firms are flexible in experimenting this way.

- Make hiring you as attractive as possible to the employer. For example, are you willing to forego some benefits that you do not really need? If married, you may be covered already on a spouse's insurance plan. If retired, you may not need an employer's contribution to a second pension. Be sure to cost out the benefits waived, so you can be compensated in salary or time off.

Regardless of the outcome, write a letter of appreciation for the interviewer's assistance and time. Remind the interviewer of how a part-time schedule can work for that particular job in that particular organization. The worst that can happen is that you will not be offered the position on a part-time basis. You have planted an idea and eventually you may be called for just the part-time opening you want.

When No Vacancy Exists

Let us say you do not have a particular employer in mind who has a part-time or a full-time professional vacancy to fill. Your task is to research the job market to ferret out prospective employers. Talk to as many part-time professionals as possible to learn how they carved out reduced work schedules.

Developing a list of employers who use your professional skills is your first order of business. Priority employers are those who already use part-time professionals or who are known in your area as innovators receptive to change. Look for the top prospects among local businesses. Take the time to evaluate the needs of local nonprofit agencies for your skills. Consider major federal installations in your area. What about local governments or the offices of state agencies? Employer targeting may take one week or six months. This information-gathering phase cannot be sidestepped because your employer list is the base for your job-search activities.

Volunteering often is valuable for the leads, experience, and references it provides. One part-time professional recalls her association with a local area council on alcoholism and drug abuse, first as a volunteer office worker, then as a board member, and always as a friend of several staff people. Eventually she gained paid employment with the agency in conference planning, proposal preparation, and data collection. If part of your motivation in accepting a volunteer position is to find paid employment, keep in mind the following:

- Do not permit the volunteer commitment to consume so much of your time and energy that you have no days left for job hunting.

- Make sure the work you are doing is relevant to your employment goals.

- Let your colleagues know that you are interested in increased responsibilities and paid employment.

Stretch your ingenuity to reach the right people who can hire you. Try to obtain an interview with the hiring officials among the employers you target. These officials may be personnel and/or operating managers. Consider carefully the following important points when approaching managers who do not know you:

- Tailor your cover letter and résumé to the requirements of the specific hiring organizations and the specific jobs you can do well.

- Sharpen your interviewing skills.

- Present yourself and the concept of part time in a confident, professional manner. Review Chapter Four for the advantages of part time and the arguments against negative questions. Be "overly" professional in your dress and demeanor.

- Demonstrate knowledge about the organization's products or services. Note how your work as a part-time professional will complement that of current employees.

- Identify your unique skills and suitability for the organization. Show what the employer will lose by not hiring you. If you are good enough, a position will be developed for you.

- Decide beforehand on the salary and responsibility levels below which you will not go. The targeted employer may be impressed with your abilities and accomplishments but offer you a lower-level part-time position and salary. Is there enough potential for you in the organization so you can accept comfortably this less professional position? If not, stand tall and politely refuse the offer. You will gain respect by so doing—and perhaps a counter offer.

Success Stories

Your determination to become a part-time professional will be tested during your job search. Do not panic if your initial contacts do not produce an immediate position. Diligence and imagination in your job search should pay off. It is essential, though, that you are well qualified professionally and up to date in your field.

Dr. Monique Cohen
Project Director, Equity Policy Center, Washington, D.C.

As project director at a nonprofit organization looking at development issues in Third World countries, Monique Cohen believes that nonprofits are fertile grounds for finding part-time professional positions. This is especially true, she suggests, for nonprofit organizations funded on a project basis.

Dr. Cohen's experience demonstrates the productivity advantages to the employer of the better qualified part-time professional. Very often, a project with limited funds can over-come its budgetary constraints by concentrating its resources on more qualified part-time professionals employed at a higher hourly cost than less skilled full-time people hired at a lower hourly cost.

New to the Washington, D.C. area in 1980, Monique Cohen first worked full time as a free-lancer. With two small children, an erratic consulting schedule did not suit her. Determined to shift to part-time work, she basically "shopped around" for an appropriate position. Confidence and determination are essential, she says, in finding part-time professional employment. Do not budge in your intentions. She eliminated many opportunities where part time was not an option.

During her job search, she spoke with the head of the Equity Policy Center, a woman she knew, about available employment. At the time, Dr. Cohen did not know about the project she ended up directing. Her credentials as a geographer and the center's needs meshed. She was hired part time.

Currently, Monique Cohen works a twenty-eight-hour week. She has experimented with different schedules, figuring out the important days and times to be at work. She settled on a four-day week of seven hours daily. Fridays are free because there are fewer meetings then. The key to a satisfactory sched-ule, she insists, is flexibility. The higher the level of your responsibility, the greater the need for flexibility. When she needs to visit her childrens' schools, she takes time off. When she travels, she works full time and either gets paid or takes "comp time."

Few people know she works part time because she always attends important meetings and conferences. Most people are "floored" when learning about her part-time schedule. Super-professional conduct, Monique Cohen believes, is the reason most "outsiders" think she is full time. Dr. Cohen recommends two major strategies for part-time professionals:

1. Find an organization with limited funding that needs your skills. Give the employer your full-time rate and negotiate yourself a part-time schedule.

2. Develop an arrangement where "nobody feels threatened or deprived."

Dean Lauver
Aeronautical Engineer, AeroStructures, Inc., Arlington, VA

Since retiring in 1980 as head of the Naval Vehicles and Weapons Division of the Office of Naval Research, Dean Lauver has enjoyed working part time for two different companies. In both cases former colleagues recruited him for his professional qualifications and accomplishments.

His first part-time opportunity arose when a colleague, retired from the Federal Aviation Agency, asked him to work on a contract awarded by the Navy to Sterling Systems, a computer firm in McLean, Virginia. Each man worked on the project half time for about 18 months, splitting the weeks between them. As Dean Lauver notes, the assignment was midway between a part-time and a job-sharing arrangement.

Two years later, another old colleague who was chief engineer for AeroStructures, an aircraft engineering firm, phoned Mr. Lauver and offered him employment. Dean Lauver's response was that he could accept only a part-time schedule. The employer agreed immediately to this request, and he started working two days per week for AeroStructures.

Both firms needed Dean Lauver's skills, so he could command the reduced work schedule he required as a retiree. Your "desirability as a part-time employee," Mr. Lauver remarks, "is a function of how well you have succeeded up to that point and the professional reputation you have built up."

Chapter Seven

Understanding Employee Benefits

Employee benefits once were called "fringe benefits." No longer a "fringe," a 1983 survey on benefits conducted by the Chamber of Commerce of the U.S. reports total employee benefits as 37 percent of payroll. This compares with four percent in 1930 and 20 percent in 1960. When considering hiring a full-time or part-time worker, the cost of employee benefits to the employer plays an important role.

Despite the steady growth of employee benefits (often called indirect compensation), part-timers often receive inadequate benefits or none at all. Since part-timers offer many advantages to employers, you should not have to forego proportionate pay or benefits for the "privilege" of working fewer hours. Neither should you be entitled to full benefits because full benefits mean excessive employer costs—reducing the number of part-time jobs.

Prorating benefits for part-time workers is equitable and easy. Benefits that are salary-linked or hours-linked are prorated automatically. You should know, too, that the Association of Part-Time Professionals supports prorated benefits for all part-time employees. Many prospective part-time employees assume that part-timers possess certain "rights" as employees which are protected by law. The fact is that most benefits are offered at the discretion of the firm. Your best policy is to inform yourself prior to negotiating with an employer about the various types of employee-benefits programs offered, know what protection is legally mandated, and understand how to prorate other benefits in order to be fairly compensated without over-burdening the employer with disproportionate costs.

One reason that the benefits issue is a complicated one for part-timers is that uniform benefits packages do not exist for private firms. In the private sector, there are vast differences in benefits programs. Even with certain common benefits like health insurance, coverage, participation, and premiums are negotiated by each firm.

In the following pages, we cover briefly the main types of indirect compensation. These are legally required benefits, payment for time not worked, and voluntary supplemental benefits. We show how to prorate benefits and when employers pay modest additional costs for employing part-time professionals.

Legally Required Benefits

Social Security and Medicare

Taxes under the Federal Insurance Contributions Act (FICA) are used to support two federally mandated programs: Old-age, Survivors, and Disability Insurance (Social Security) and Hospital Insurance (Medicare). These programs fall under the jurisdiction of the U.S. Department of Health and Human Services. Employers, employees, and the self-employed pay contributions during their working years which finance benefits to current recipients and administrative costs of operating the programs.

One out of six Americans receives monthly Social Security checks, and over ninety percent of workers earn protection under the system. As of January 1, 1984, employees of nonprofit organizations and new federal employees must be covered. Termination of state and local government Social Security coverage is prohibited. Employers and employees pay equal amounts to cover these programs at the rates shown below.

Table 4. Social Security Taxes

Year	Tax Rate			Maximum Taxable Earnings*
	Social Security	Medicare	Total	
1985	5.70	1.35	7.05	$39,600
1986–7	5.70	1.45	7.15	
1988–9	6.06	1.45	7.51	
1990–	6.20	1.45	7.65	

*Rises each year with cost of living increases as measured by the Consumer Price Index, provided there is an automatic benefit increase.

Two part-timers cost an employer more than one full-time employee for FICA taxes only for jobs with a salary above the maximum taxable earnings (in 1985, $39,600). For a $50,000 job at the 1985 tax rate of 7.05 percent, the increase in FICA taxes to the employer for using two part-timers would be $733.

Unemployment Insurance

Unemployment Insurance (UI) is a federal-state program designed to provide temporary income to the unemployed while they seek work. The U.S. Department of Labor administers the federal portion, and employment commissions operate in each state. Within the federal framework, each state has the authority to set its own benefit structure, eligibility requirements, and financing methods.

Taxes assessed solely to the employer by both the federal and state governments finance unemployment compensation. In 1985, the effective tax rate was .8 percent of the first $7,000 earned. This money is used to administer the state programs and to provide a loan fund for states that deplete their own reserves. During recessions, the federal government becomes more involved through extended and supplemental programs.

State taxes are converted directly into payments for the unemployed. Employers' taxes vary widely, even within the same state. A firm receives a tax rate based on its experience rating, which is computed from previous withdrawals from the company's unemployment fund. Each state sets its own rules for determining the experience rating. Check with the firms in which you are interested to find their exact tax rates.

Employers who hire two part-time professionals instead of one full-time worker pay the UI taxes twice. In a state where the taxable wage base is $8,000, the employer pays taxes on the first $8,000 of one full-time employee earning $20,000. The same employer would pay taxes on $16,000 for two employees earning $10,000 each. The federal tax is minimal, at most $56 per employee per year. As we have seen, the amount of the state tax for unemployment compensation depends on the individual firm's rate. If a firm has a high rate because of large past withdrawals, cost considerations might reduce the incentives to employ sizeable numbers of part-time professionals.

Workers' Compensation

Workers' Compensation (WC) is a state system with no federal counterpart. Although the program is not uniform, its general intent is to make employers financially liable for accidents occurring at the work place or illnesses arising from industrial conditions. Claims are heard by a board or taken to court.

Regulations and benefits vary greatly among states. Benefits to the injured or ill worker may include medical coverage, partial wages, rehabilitation, and/or survivor allowances due to time lost from work. Coverage usually is handled through private insurance firms. Part-time and full-time employees are covered on the same basis. Premiums for part-time employees are prorated automatically, costing the employer no additional money.

State Disability Insurance

Unrelated to workers' compensation, five states also require employers to pay for a state disability insurance program for their employees. This short-term, nonoccupational disability program covers off-the-job accidents and illnesses. The plans provide partial income for a limited period (usually twenty-six weeks). Premiums usually are tied to salaries, making part-timers no more expensive than other workers. The states involved are California, Hawaii, New Jersey, New York, and Rhode Island.

Payment for Time Not Worked

Vacations, holidays, and sick leave are the major types of payments for time not worked. Others include personal leave, jury and military duty, and sabbaticals. The most equitable way to handle vacations for a part-timer is to prorate vacations according to the policy for full-time counterparts. If a forty-hour per week employee receives twenty days of vacation, the employee working thirty hours per week should obtain fifteen days of vacation time and the half-time employee, ten days. While this example is simple mathematically, fractional days or hours should not present a problem.

Holidays for part-timers can be prorated as vacations. This may entail a switch in schedule of a full-day, part-week employee needing to "make up" some time or an adjustment in salary if part of the holiday is given without pay. Part-day, full-week employees automatically have the benefit prorated. Another option practiced by the federal government and many other employers is giving the holiday to all regularly scheduled workers. In these cases, many part-timers choose Monday as one of their regularly scheduled work days.

Sick leave policy varies among firms. Most policies are built around some sort of accrual system, facilitating prorating for part-timers. If a full-time employee accrues eight hours of sick leave per month, half-timers receive four. Vacation and sick leave often are linked to seniority, granting workers with more years of service an increasing amount of time. Where the primary purpose is blocking high-turnover personnel from participating in benefit plans, the hours worked each week should not make a difference. In other cases, employees earn benefits by the number of years of service. Seniority can be prorated, with half-time workers requiring two years to equal one year of service for their full-time counterparts. If the benefits are prorated, then the length of service should not be.

Voluntary Supplemental Benefits

Group Insurance

Major providers of group insurance policies are private insurance companies, Blue Cross/Blue Shield, health maintenance organizations, and self-funded plans. Disability and life insurance policies normally are salary-linked, leading to prorated premiums for part-timers. Maternity leave, by law, must be treated as any other disability.

Health and dental insurance usually have standard coverage with two premium rates, for the single or family policy. Confronted by escalating costs, some companies are experimenting with premiums for married couples with no children, or different rates based on the number of children. Some large employers offer different insurance plans with varying levels of coverage and costs. This, however, is rare.

Inflexibility in the types of health and dental coverage means that part-timers must negotiate with the employer about splitting their premiums. Many full-time workers also contribute toward their insurance coverage. As companies seek to contain costs, the trend is toward more employees paying higher percentages of the cost of their policies. Prorate the premium, figure your share of the cost, and decide whether to participate in the insurance program. If you already are covered under another plan, it may not be necessary to have two policies.

One other aspect of health insurance concerns part-time employees. A common practice limits group insurance to full-time people (defined as those working at least thirty hours per week). Insurance companies do this to avoid temporary employees with medical problems who may work for a short time solely to become eligible for insurance. This thirty-hour requirement is not mandated by law but is an attempt by insurance companies to protect themselves. Insurers usually are willing to waive this requirement for permanent part-time employees.

Pension Plans

Retirement plans are not legally required. If an employer chooses to provide a pension plan, however, the plan usually must conform to the Employee Retirement Income Security Act (ERISA) of 1974. Exempt from ERISA are government plans; certain church plans; plans maintained solely to comply with disability, unemployment, or workers' compensation laws; and plans maintained outside the United States primarily for nonresident aliens.

ERISA contains one very important sentence for part-time employees. Retirement coverage must be provided to all employees twenty-one years of age, with one year of service, who work 1,000 hours or more per year (approximately half time). The 1,000 hours could be twenty hours per week or six months full time. If the plan provides immediate, full vesting, the length of service may be extended to three years. Other provisions of this complicated 208-page law provide more liberal standards of eligibility.

Early pension plans and those still used in most large firms are called defined benefit plans. In these plans, the employee's annuity upon retirement is fixed. Contributions are determined by estimating the necessary investment to reap the promised benefit. Defined benefit plans are subject to all the rules of ERISA, including plan insurance. They offer some financial certainty to employees, but cost uncertainty to employers.

Most recent pension plans are defined contribution plans. These are account plans for individual employees where the employer's contribution is predetermined. The annuity payable at retirement is whatever money has accumulated in the employee's account. Employers are not subject to many ERISA requirements regarding insurance or funding. The employee has no assured, specific retirement income and bears the responsibility for investing contributions.

Premiums for both types of pension plans usually are tied to earnings, again prorating costs for part-timers. Annuities under defined benefit plans are linked to seniority and usually are based on the highest or last three to five years of earnings times the number of years of service.

Other Benefits

Numerous other employee benefits are available to American workers, including vision insurance, prepaid legal plans, child care reimbursement, educational assistance, bonuses, and discounts. These less common benefits usually can be prorated. Executive "perks"—company cars, personal financial planning, and stock options—probably will not be offered to part-timers even at professional levels.

Flexible Benefits

Flexible benefits programs, often referred to as "cafeteria-style benefits," are a recent development which may set the standard for benefits administration in the future. Some plans start with a minimal core of benefits that all employees receive and add flexible credits to buy optional coverage. Flexible credits are offered on the basis of salary or years of service. Other plans offer different levels of the same benefit. Most companies with flexible benefits programs permit employees to change the benefit mix annually.

Today, over 150 firms covering three million workers have some form of cafeteria benefits. The firms include:

TRW, Inc.

Educational Testing Service

Eastman Kodak Company

Xerox Corporation

American Can Company

Honeywell, Inc.

PepsiCo, Inc.

Mellon National Corporation

Marriott Corporation

Quaker Oats Company

Texaco, Inc.

The growth of these plans is great news for part-timers. More options and different levels of coverage make it easier for you to negotiate and design an equitable benefits package. Since the employer already is tailoring benefits for the full-time work force, your request will not be novel.

Issues and Outlook for Part-Timers

Part-timers should be aware of other benefits issues which may affect them. These issues include eligibility for unemployment compensation, maternity leave, and pension rights; impact of post-retirement earnings on Social Security and on private pensions; deterrents to phased retirement under current pension formulas; and the changing character of the labor force.

- Some part-time employees find themselves ineligible for unemployment compensation, if unemployed, even though their employers paid the relevant taxes. This is due to certain state requirements about attachment to the labor force. While many states have minimal requirements, others may exclude permanent part-timers with low earnings or free–lancers who have not worked a certain number of continuous weeks. Also, most states require that the claimant be actively seeking work and accept any job offered which is at a comparable skill level. If a former part-timer is offered a full-time job and turns it down solely because of hours, benefits may be denied.

- A woman who takes extended maternity leave must check her company's retirement policy to see how a break in service affects pension rights. It is possible she could lose many years of credit. Legislation passed in 1984 protects the rights of women who leave the work force temporarily.

- Most retirees who choose to work want to do so on a part-time basis. There are financial considerations concerning how the additional income will affect retirement annuities and tax status. Private pensions frequently are diminished when the annuitant works. Earned income also affects Social Security benefits. Above the allowable income, one dollar out of every two dollars of Social Security benefits is withheld. This percentage changes to one dollar out of every three in 1990. The allowable income limit in 1985 is $5,400 for an individual below age sixty-five, $7,320 for those sixty-five to sixty-nine, and no limit for people aged seventy and above. The income limit will increase yearly.

  Retired professionals who do return to work part time will be affected by the tax implications of the 1983 Social Security amendments. Up to one-half of Social Security benefits now are subject to federal income tax if annuitants exceed stipulated levels of income.

- Many individuals would prefer phased retirement to abruptly ending a long working life. Current pension policy discourages phasing down at work because annuities usually are based on the highest or last three-to-five-year earnings period. If your pension is figured on your last years of earnings, you would be reluctant to cut back hours during that time. Even if it is based on your highest three to five years of salary (which may have occurred several years before), the value of your annuity would have declined because of the inflation factor in the intervening time.

  In contrast, pension plans benefit individuals who choose to work part time in mid-career. Conceivably, you could work part time for thirty-five years and full time for the final five years of your career. Your annuities then would equal those of a full-time employee with forty years seniority.

- Benefits packages are changing to reflect upheavals in the labor force. Programs designed for the "traditional" family (a male breadwinner with a wife at home and dependent children) are no longer appropriate for everyone. More women in the work place, earlier retirement, single-parent families, and other changes dictate new ways of looking at compensation.

Increasing flexibility in employee benefits means a more receptive environment when you are attempting to negotiate indirect compensation. "Cafeteria-style benefits" and defined contribution pension plans offer special advantages to the part-time professional. Use this new flexibility to tailor a benefits package that fits your needs and makes the employer happy. Negotiating an equitable benefits package requires you to:

1. Know the facts. Part-time professionals cost more to the employer than full-timers only in taxes for unemployment insurance. FICA taxes are more costly for the limited number of high-skill jobs that pay above the maximum taxable earnings.

2. Gather information on the details of your targeted firm's benefits.

3. Work up a proposal that prorates benefits or exchanges them to meet your requirements. Be sure that your proposal will not cost the employer additional money. If you choose to waive certain benefits, ask for more salary or vacation time. A written proposal that reflects good research and a desire for equitable compensation marks you as a serious professional.

Exercise 9:

Cost Analysis for Employee Benefits

When you do a cost comparison, you cannot compare apples and oranges. You must analyze the proposed benefits of your part-time job against a full-time job with comparable job duties and salary.

What is the employer's $ contribution for a full-time employee?	What would the employer's $ contribution be for you as a part-timer?
Legally required benefits	*Legally required benefits*
FICA _____	FICA _____
UI _____	UI _____
WC _____	WC _____
State disability _____	State disability _____
Voluntary benefits	*Voluntary benefits*
Health insurance _____	Health insurance _____
Life insurance _____	Life insurance _____
Dental insurance _____	Dental insurance _____
Disability insurance _____	Disability insurance _____
Retirement _____	Retirement _____
Other _____	Other _____
_____	_____
_____	_____
Total _____	Total _____

What is the percentage of your total compared
to the full-time worker? _____

What is the percentage of your hours
compared to the full-time worker? _____

The percentage of the employer's contribution should not exceed
the percentage of your hours worked. Remember, all time off
with pay can be prorated and should not show up as a $
contribution by the employer.

Unfortunately, some employers refuse to include individuals
working less than full time in their benefits program. If you
have access to plans through former employment or via your
spouse, this may not be crucial to you. However, many people
are not covered elsewhere, and the cost of buying insurance
coverage on a single basis may be prohibitive.

One option is to see if your employer will cover you under
the firm's group policy if you agree to pay the entire premium.
This may not seem fair, but you still will be better off than
trying to find policies on your own. Another possibility is to
check into group coverage elsewhere. Professional associations, clubs, and even credit cards offer various types of group
plans. Their rates will not be as good as employer sponsored
programs, but will be lower than single coverage.

If you end up paying for your own insurance and retirement
plans, make certain you take advantage of tax deductions. IRA
and Keogh deposits are tax deductible, as are medical expenses
(including insurance premiums) over a certain amount. A tax
credit also is given for a percentage of child care expenses.

Chapter Eight

Learning to Negotiate

Negotiation skills are important for all professionals when seeking a job and when on the job. For part-time professionals, negotiation skills are critical. You may be a pioneer in the firm; the firm usually will have no policy at all, and the deal you work out may become standard policy for future part-timers. Salary, benefits, hours, schedules, and job responsibilities are some areas open to negotiation. Bargaining most often occurs in the private sector. Government positions, in comparison, are standardized—with fixed salary ranges.

Among private firms and nonprofit organizations, there is always room to bargain. For higher-level jobs, the chances increase that bargaining will take place. In fact, most employers expect to negotiate. If you accept the first offer, a prospective employer may be disappointed. The employer may think that you would have accepted anything or that you may not be very good after all.

Your Attitude is Important

Many part-time professionals feel so "fortunate" to be discussing a responsible job that they fear questioning initial offers. Remember the advantages that you bring to the employer. These advantages warrant a prorated salary and benefits package.

Recognize that salary is a measure of professional status and competence. Remember too that your commitment to the job and the organization may be questioned. If you accept a salary clearly out of line with your professional attainments and the compensation of co-workers performing equivalent tasks, you will be reinforcing the attitude that part-timers are second-class workers. Do not be surprised if you wind up resenting your situation.

Be sure to include benefits as part of your total compensation package. You may not need all the standard benefits if they duplicate coverage through a spouse or a retirement package. Cost out the benefits you waive and negotiate for replacement compensation—more salary, vacation, etc. If you have agreed to a trial period of employment with no benefits included, take the time to develop a benefits proposal in case the employment becomes permanent.

Clearly understanding your own needs for salary and benefits is the first step in negotiating a compensation package. Flexibility is very important since part-time professionals are such rare birds in many organizations. Do not be rigid but adhere to a minimum compensation package below which you will not go.

Do Your Homework

Some research is important before you get into a negotiating situation. Make sure you know what your market value is. You can obtain this information from the following sources:

- Friends and business acquaintances. They may not divulge their own salaries but probably will be happy to talk about others or make general comments.

- Trade publications. These magazines often run articles that give information on the latest trends in employment.

- Salary surveys. Many industries conduct their own salary surveys of sample companies. The U.S. Department of Labor also produces reports on standard salaries and benefits in firms.

- <u>Want ads.</u> Many employment ads do not specify salaries but quite often give a salary range.

- <u>Professional and trade associations.</u> One purpose of these associations is to gather information on members which then is used to help firms and individuals set compensation.

- <u>Executive recruiters.</u> Search firms know the going rates for various occupations.

Accurately assessing the negotiating environment is equally important. You always do not have as much information as you would like, but you must judge as wisely as you can how much leverage you do have. Negotiating means give and take. Probably you will not get everything you want. Decide, from the negotiating environment, how likely it is that certain demands will be met:

- <u>Does the employer really want you or are there five other equally qualified candidates?</u> (Asking about the competition and the employer's selection process are both valid questions for an applicant to broach.)

- <u>Is there time pressure on the employer?</u> (Managers backed up with work or facing important deadlines can be very accommodating.)

- <u>Are there special factors to be considered?</u> (Are you, for example, the chairman of the board's son-in-law?)

Rules for Negotiating

The primary purpose of an initial interview is to exchange information about job responsibilities and applicant skills. After these areas are explored thoroughly, you then talk about the specifics of employment—pay, hours, benefits, schedule, etc. These specifics may be most important to you, but they are not to the employer. The worst response to an employer's request for questions about the job are detail-oriented inquiries. Do not ask, for example, about free parking. Keep in mind the following rules. Remember that negotiating extends beyond the discussion of salary:

- Never bring up the specifics first. Always allow the employer to shift the conversation to the terms of employment.

- Have a target in mind. Set boundaries ahead of time and do not stray too far off base. It is easy to be swayed during the interview and to go along with another's suggestions.

- Evade incriminating questions. Giving numbers to a question like: "What is the minimum you will accept?" is dangerous. Give a general response: "It would depend on the job responsibilities, benefits, and other factors," or "I would need some time to analyze all the considerations."

- Pin down the employer on details. You are in a better position if you can get the employer to name a salary range first. Then, you will not sell yourself cheaply.

- Go for the top. If a salary range is stated, go for the highest figure and confine all further references to that amount.

- Focus on yourself as an asset to the company. Do not discuss your needs. Talk about your value to the company.

- Combine factors when negotiating. If your salary demands seem too high, for example, try to increase the responsibilities of the job.

- Consider trial employment. Offer to work a trial period to prove you are worth the price you are asking.

- Think about the future. Include in your discussion, where possible, timetables for future raises and promotions.

- Do not overlook the intangibles. A job is more than compensation. Consider other advantages. Will you be receiving valuable training to enhance your career? Are the contacts you will make helpful? Is this a prestigious job that will look good on your résumé?

- Think it over. Do not hesitate to take twenty-four hours to consider a final offer. The input from friends and some quiet time away from the interview can be invaluable.

Job Contracts

Once the negotiations are completed, try to obtain some written documentation of the basic points of your agreement. Mutual understanding between you and your employer at the beginning will avoid on-the-job problems. A job contract signed by both parties offers the most legal protection, but many firms are unwilling to sign written agreements. An alternative is to outline in an acceptance letter what you understand to be the terms of your employment. Consult the following checklist for job contract basics:

- Salary. Is your salary prorated? Is overtime or compensatory time available if your part-time hours are exceeded? How are you paid—straight salary or hourly rates?

- Employee benefits. What types of programs are available to you? Are they prorated? Do you pay some of the premium on insurance policies?

- Job responsibilities. Are your duties clearly outlined? Are deadlines involved which need to be specified?

- Work schedule. Do you work a set schedule each week? Are your hours constant regardless of work load? Must you be available on your days off for meetings in the office or consultations via the phone? Are you compensated for this time?

- Advancement opportunities. Do you have access to training programs or tuition reimbursement? Are there opportunities for promotion?

- Firing rights. Are part-timers let go before others in times of cutbacks? Is there advance notification and severance compensation?

After negotiating your initial job arrangement, you cannot just breathe a sigh of relief and relax. Negotiation takes place constantly on the job regarding raises, promotions, job assignments, and other matters. Put your skills to use and bargain for what you want.

Exercise 10:

You are negotiating an employment agreement. Practice with a friend and alternate the part of Applicant and Employer. Set a time limit (fifteen minutes) during which you must reach an agreement.

After your negotiation answer the following questions:

a) How did you do on

hours_____

schedule_____

salary_____

benefits_____

b) What was difficult for you? Do you need to alter your style somewhat? Remember, negotiation involves at least two different personalities. The process changes with each pair of individuals.

Applicant

You have applied for a job as a writer/editor for the National Association of Computer Addicts. This is a new, growing association with 10,000 members. It currently employs four staff members—the executive director, a software researcher, and two clericals. You are at your second interview and can tell the executive director wants to hire you. You think the job sounds perfect and will give you an opportunity to learn and possibly advance as the organization grows. As you begin to discuss the details of your employment keep in mind the following goals:

HOURS You would like to work twenty hours per week and can not possibly manage more than twenty-four hours in an office each week.

SCHEDULE You know the only cost effective way for you to work is no more than three days per week.

SALARY You would like to make $12 per hour and have set $10 as your bottom line.

BENEFITS Your spouse is self-employed and you need health insurance. Anything else you can get would be nice. You learn that the full-time employees get vacation, sick leave, holidays, health insurance, life insurance, disability insurance, and retirement.

Employer

You are the executive director of the National Association of Computer Addicts. Your two-year old organization has 10,000 members and is growing rapidly. Your current staff includes a full-time software researcher, two secretaries, and yourself. You need a writer/editor to perform the following functions: put out a monthly newsletter, press releases, annual directory, and other publications. You have interviewed several candidates but one is outstanding. As you negotiate the employment details, here are your goals:

HOURS   You would like to have the individual work approximately thirty hours per week.

SCHEDULE   You prefer the individual to be in on a daily basis, i.e., five days for six hours per day.

SALARY   You think you can afford about $8–$10 per hour. Obviously, the lower, the better.

BENEFITS   You have never had a part-timer before and do not know what is expected. You are willing to give some vacation, sick leave, and holidays, but are not sure how much. The association provides health insurance, disability insurance, life insurance, and defined contribution retirement for the four full-time employees. You would just as soon not mess with including part-timers in these plans.

Chapter Nine

Government Agencies as Employers

"Forget it. Why bother? There's too much red tape. Besides, few openings exist for part-time professionals at any level of government."

Do the above sentiments express your attitude toward government employment? If so, our advice is not to ignore government if you want part-time work. Although government agencies have special characteristics that distinguish them from private sector employers, many reasons for employing part-time professionals apply to employers across the board. Reviewing the ten special characteristics of private sector employers receptive to part-time professionals (discussed in Chapter Three), we note a number equally applicable to government agencies:

- Government employs large numbers of professionals in traditional part-time occupations. Examples are librarians, psychologists, teachers, and health care professionals.

- Government competes for scarce talent in the same kinds of specialties as private firms. Examples are engineers, systems analysts, and medical personnel.

- Government agencies almost exclusively are service organizations.

- Government, like private sector employers, increasingly has women in top management positions.

- Many aspects of government operations involve high technology.

- Government agencies, regardless of mission, certainly are socially conscious. Increasing employment opportunities for targeted groups are major reasons for government legislation and directives to promote part time. These targeted groups include parents, older workers, the handicapped, and students.

Federal Government

"It's nice work if you can get it," goes the old refrain. Working for the federal government has many advantages. The pay is good and benefits are equitable for part-timers. However, entering the federal government as a part-time professional is not easy during times of expansion, and it is nearly impossible during slowdowns and cutbacks. Converting from full-time to part-time work is now the best way for professionals to gain permanent part-time status.

Although the numbers are small, part-time professional employment is rising in the federal government. Consider the steady growth in career part-time employees serving in middle management or professional slots. The numbers tell the story.

Table 5.
Part-Time Employees, GS-10 and above

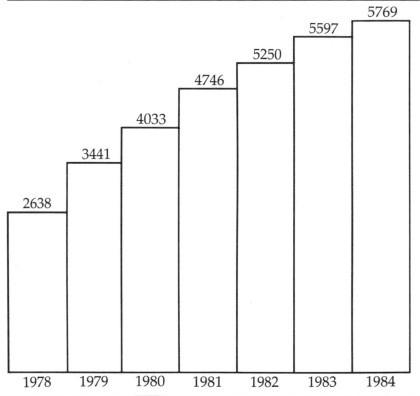

1978	1979	1980	1981	1982	1983	1984
2638	3441	4033	4746	5250	5597	5769

Occupations with most part-time professional employees include medical officer, nurse, social insurance administrator, computer specialist, and educational and vocational training. Significant numbers of part-time professionals also can be found in social science, social work, personnel management, program analysis, and chemistry.

Also illustrating the wide range of part-time professional positions available are the hundreds of federal listings processed through the job referral service of the Association of Part-Time Professionals in the Washington, D.C. area. Examples are:

- Accountant/Auditor
- Administrative Officer

- Attorney
- Budget Analyst
- Computer Programmer
- Contracts Specialist
- Economist
- Education Program Specialist
- Employee Development Specialist
- Environmental Protection Specialist
- Equal Employment Opportunity Specialist
- Librarian
- Management Analyst
- Personnel Management Specialist
- Position Classification Specialist
- Program Analyst
- Public Information Specialist
- Social Science Analyst
- Statistician
- Systems Analyst

Part-time programs are mandated by law in the federal government. The Federal Employees Part-Time Career Employment Act, passed in 1978, provided a major impetus to part-time employment. Congress examined the benefits to the federal government as an employer and found them to be increased productivity and job satisfaction, lower turnover and absenteeism, and enhanced management flexibility. Key provisions of the federal part-time legislation follow:

- Narrows the definition of part-time career employment from scheduled work of less than forty hours per week to scheduled work between sixteen and thirty-two hours per week, for employees who became part time after April 8, 1979.

- Requires agencies to establish, by regulation, programs to expand part-time career employment opportunities in competitive and excepted positions at grade levels through GS-15 or equivalent. Agency programs must include annual goals and timetables for establishing part-time positions.

- Requires agencies to report twice each year to the Office of Personnel Management on progress in meeting part-time career employment goals together with an explanation of impediments experienced in meeting such goals and measures taken to overcome them.

- Changes the current method for determining personnel ceilings in each agency by requiring the counting of part-time employees on the basis of the fractional part of the forty-hour week actually worked (effective October 1, 1980).

- Prorates the government contribution for the health insurance of eligible employees who became part time on or after April 8, 1979, on the basis of the fraction of a full-time schedule worked.

State and Local Government

State and local governments are particularly good sources of employment for part-time professionals. In fact, they often are the largest employers of human services professionals in many communities. Until recently, both full-time and part-time employment has been expanding in state and local government agencies. Currently, some areas are cutting back due to declining populations, tax restrictions, and reduced federal aid. Hiring freezes, though, are temporary.

New York is a striking example of one state taking the initiative on part–time employment. The Part-Time/Shared Job Project is part of the Department of Civil Service, the central personnel agency for the state's 165,000 jobs. About 7,000 employees in New York state government work part time and several thousand more are considering reduced work schedules. Professionals comprise one-third of this part-time work force.

Managers in New York State uniformly give high marks to the performance of part-time employees in level of skills, job commitment, and labor fatigue and stress on the job. Evaluating part-time professionals, most New York State managers saw their productivity, absenteeism, tardiness, and turnover as no different or better than full-time professionals.

Local governments often have a higher percentage of part-timers than their state counterparts. Many local governments are so small that they rely almost entirely on part-time staff. Large municipal systems have a good record on hiring part-timers. There are also multi-county or city organizations set up to manage joint governmental projects. The hiring process is handled by the joint agency, with salary and benefits reflecting a mixture of the governments represented.

State and local government agencies in northern Virginia, Maryland, and the District of Columbia list many part-time professional vacancies with the Association of Part-Time Professionals' job referral service in that area. Examples of openings are:

- Career Counselor
- Community Coordinator
- Computer Programmer
- Human Services Administrator
- Instructor
- Job Developer
- Librarian
- Mental Health Therapist
- Nurse
- Personnel Specialist
- Program Analyst
- Psychologist
- Public Information Officer
- Recreation Leader
- Rehabilitation/Vocational Counselor

- Research Assistant
- Speech Therapist
- Social Worker
- Substance Abuse Counselor
- Systems Analyst
- Teacher
- Trainer
- Urban Planner
- Volunteer Coordinator
- Writer/Editor

Do not ignore educational institutions at both the local and state levels. Public schools obviously employ many part-time teachers. Equally important, they use other human services professionals and administrators on a part-time basis. Adult education programs, staffed almost entirely by part-timers, are often a separate entity in larger counties. Public colleges and universities, usually part of huge state systems, employ significant numbers of part-time faculty each semester plus many permanent part-timers in nonteaching areas.

Two school systems that have turned to part-timers to save administrative costs report excellent results. In Kansas, five percent of Wichita's public school teachers work on a part-time basis, receiving prorated salaries and benefits. Legislation passed in 1978 allowed employees to retire at age sixty, receive pensions, and return to work on a part-time basis. The director of employment relations cites two major advantages to the program—the ability to hire more new teachers and the wonderful training provided by the more experienced teachers to the younger ones.

San Francisco's school district estimates saving several millions of dollars by allowing teachers to cut back on hours. Three plans are available to San Francisco's teachers. The "Early Retirement Consultant" plan allows teachers over age fifty with ten years' experience to receive reduced pensions and consult with the school district on a part-time basis. Older workers also may continue teaching half time and receive a reduced pension plus prorated salary. Finally, all certified teachers have the option of working on a half-time basis. In all these cases, retirement annuities and benefits are calculated on full-time salaries.

Official Policies and Programs

A survey conducted for the National Council of Alternative Work Patterns shows that at least thirty-five states have programs for permanent part-timers. Six of these have enacted legislation mandating part-time employment (see chart below). In several others, executive orders or statewide personnel directives encourage part-time initiatives. Listed below are the states in which at least one agency employs individuals on a permanent part-time basis. States which have passed legislation permitting or encouraging the use of permanent part-time employment are marked with an asterisk (*).

Alaska	Missouri
Arizona	Montana
California	Nebraska
Colorado	New York
Georgia	North Carolina
Hawaii	Ohio
Idaho	Oklahoma
Illinois*	Oregon
Iowa	Pennsylvania
Kansas	Rhode Island
Kentucky	South Dakota
Louisiana	Utah
Maine	Vermont
Maryland*	Virginia*
Massachusetts*	Washington
Michigan	West Virginia
Minnesota	Wisconsin*
Mississippi	

Do not assume that laws or policy directives from on high automatically translate into part-time jobs, particularly at the professional level. What legislative support does is to give you leverage with government managers and some assurance that official rules and regulations have been drafted to carry out the law. In most cases, too, there will be a part-time program and a personnel specialist in the government agency who follows the part-time program. This personnel specialist is called a part-time coordinator in the federal government.

The State of Maryland provides an example of good intentions on the subject of part-time employment going awry. In 1975, legislation required the executive branch of the state government to provide part-time opportunities for those unable to work full time. The law established prorated benefits and adjusted personnel ceilings. Part-time quotas were set—yearly increases from one percent to a maximum of five percent at all grade levels. In fact, the legislative goals have not been reached and part-timers are found disproportionately in lower-grade levels.

Pilot Programs at the State Level

Pilot programs initiated by state governments have documented the advantages to the employer of part-timers. These programs also provide a model for the effective utilization of reduced-hour employees in large organizations. Massachusetts passed the first legislation in 1974 mandating alternative work schedules. Part-timers working half time or more received employee benefits, and state agencies were required to increase their part-time work force. While the original numerical goals were not met, a five-year evaluation yielded the following results:

- Any job can be done on a part-time basis.
- No single characteristic of a job, including supervising others, prevents a job from being done on a part-time basis.
- Other staff members do not resent part-timers.
- Most part-timers are flexible and are willing to be available occasionally on their off hours. Part-timers showed real commitment.
- Success of the part-time arrangement depended greatly on managers' attitudes.

- Part-time opportunities opened up job possibilities for women and older workers.

- Part-time employees demonstrated higher morale and had lower absenteeism and turnover rates.

Project JOIN was a federally-funded research and demonstration project conducted jointly with the Wisconsin state government in the mid-1970's. Its purpose was to test job sharing and flexible work arrangements in the Wisconsin Civil Service. The project surveyed 28,000 state employees and found that three percent expressed an immediate need for permanent part-time employment.

Forty-five full-time professional and paraprofessional jobs were marked as suitable for job sharing. The positions studied included attorneys, medical technologists, and social workers. Project results showed increased job satisfaction, higher productivity, no significant cost increase, lower turnover and sick leave, and an enhanced affirmative action program. Most important, the evaluations demonstrated that part time can work in professional situations. Today, permanent part-time employment is used widely in Wisconsin state agencies, accounting for seven percent of the total work force. Legislation passed in 1978 directed expansion of part-time and other flexible work schedules.

California employs more than 3,000 workers on a permanent part-time basis, mainly in clerical positions. Agencies note the following advantages of their part-time work force—better retention, improved worker attitudes, flexibility in changing workloads, and a larger pool of trained employees.

A two-year pilot program conducted in the Department of Motor Vehicles (DMV) in 1977 contributed to the growing interest in part time among California state agencies. The DMV recommended expansion of the part-time program, provided that managers and supervisors controlled the decisions to make individual jobs part time. Advantages noted by the DMV study were:

- Help in meeting affirmative action goals.

- Decreased unemployment and overtime costs.

- Greater productivity, increased job satisfaction, and improved quality of work life.

Disadvantages cited were increased costs and slower promotions for part-time employees.

As you can see from this chapter, government agencies are impressive employers of part-time professionals. Now, you ask, "How do I secure part-time employment with a government agency in my area?" For that information, please turn to the next chapter.

Chapter Ten

Working for Government as a Part-Time Professional

Your employer-targeting strategy for government, as for private employers, depends on your current employment status. Do you work full time for the government, or do you want to enter from the outside? The best part-time opportunities are for professionals who now work full time and wish to convert to part time in their present agencies. It is more difficult to come in cold from the outside.

We focus in this chapter on the special characteristics of government that you, as a prospective part-time professional, must know about. Relevant information contained in Chapters Five and Six—on converting your full-time job to part time, and on obtaining a part-time job as an outsider—will not be repeated. We cover here only additional information that is specifically applicable to professionals seeking part-time positions in government service.

Personnel Ceilings

Budgets and the availability of funds at all levels of government determine whether there will be increased hiring or reductions-in-force. Another constraint, peculiar to government, are their personnel ceiling systems. It is crucial for you, as a prospective part-time professional, to understand how the personnel ceiling system works. The basics are not complicated and they apply to all government agencies.

Top managers at each government agency generally receive personnel allocations for their agencies from political officials and the central personnel office. These agency personnel allocations then are divided among the different operating and staff subdivisions of the agency. These personnel allocations are the personnel ceilings, and they determine the personnel mix in the agency from top to bottom. There are two broad types of personnel ceiling systems:

1. The "body count" system is one whereby personnel ceilings are set in terms of the number of people working. This system works against the employment of part-time people because a part-time employee is counted as one employee for personnel ceiling purposes. Under a "body count" system, managers gain more by hiring full-time people.

2. More favorable to part-time employment is the second type of personnel ceiling system that emphasizes the hours people work rather than the number of people working. This system often is known as a "full-time equivalent" (FTE) system. Under the FTE system, two part-timers, each working twenty hours per week, are equal to one full-time person working forty hours per week. Each twenty–hour person counts, for personnel ceiling purposes, as one-half of a full-time employee. Managers do not lose by employing part-timers under an FTE or "fractional" counting system.

Today, in the federal government, all full-time and part-time people are under a single personnel ceiling system based on full-time equivalence (FTE). Now federal managers can think in terms of hours of work instead of number of bodies. Managers can easily interchange full-time and part-time personnel. Since the current federal personnel ceiling system is fairly new, some federal managers still may be under the erroneous assumption that they need to count personnel rather than hours and work years. Sometimes, it takes official policy a while to trickle down to operating levels. Remind federal managers about the new personnel ceiling system and let them know that they can expect good productivity from employing permanent part-time people.

Although it is difficult to generalize about fifty state governments and thousands of local ones, it is a fact that they all operate under some kind of personnel ceiling system. Find out whether the particular agency you wish to work for operates under the "body count" or the "FTE" system. Selling managers on part time will be much easier if your targeted state or local government agencies operate under the "FTE" type of personnel ceiling system.

Converting Your Full-Time Job to Part Time

The federal government is particularly receptive to professional employees reducing their work schedules. Almost one-third of members of the Association of Part-Time Professionals in the Washington, D.C. area reported, in a survey, that they obtained their federal part-time positions by first working full time for the federal government and then converting to part time. For the first time in 1983, a majority of all new part-time workers (outside the Postal Service) were conversions of current federal employees.

If you are currently a full-time state or local government employee, you probably are in a good position to convert your job to part time. Where part time is encouraged, you may encounter no resistance at all. The approval of your immediate supervisor will be key.

The ease of conversion in the federal government depends mostly upon your agency's implementation of the Federal Employees Part-Time Career Employment Act and your supervisor's attitude. For every success story, there is a frustrated individual who has given up because of stubborn agency opposition or has switched back to full time due to constant pressure from superiors. Remember that frustration occurs in the private sector as well. Be persistent and do not give up until you have exhausted every possibility.

In the federal government, your agency's part-time coordinator should be of assistance. The part-time coordinator is responsible for your agency's program to promote part-time employment, a program mandated by the federal part-time law. Obtain copies of your agency's regulations on part-time work, published in the Code of Federal Regulations or as an internal agency document. Ask to see the written procedures for converting full-time positions to part time and the reports sent to the Office of Personnel Management twice yearly on the agency's progress in meeting annual goals for part-time employment.

After investigating your agency's rules and regulations, you must speak to as many part-time professionals as possible. As in the private sector, these conversations will help you to judge actual agency practice regarding part time. Your next step is to analyze your job thoroughly so you can negotiate realistically and successfully with your supervisor. Show your boss that you are familiar with the provisions of the federal part-time law, know the procedures for conversion to part time, and can explain how part-timers are accounted for under the full-time equivalent (FTE) personnel ceiling system.

Among large employers with formal and codified personnel systems—and certainly in the federal government—there is an option for individuals to work part time and to retain their status as permanent full-time employees. Under this option, you can propose a "leave without pay" situation where you work and are paid for part-time hours but continue officially as a full-time permanent employee. This approach may be desirable if you seek to convert to part time for a relatively short period.

If your supervisor agrees to your conversion to part-time hours, there still may be necessary paperwork to complete. In the federal government particularly, there will be special forms requesting conversion to part time and supplemental written statements explaining the reasons for your request and the advantages to the agency. Do not neglect this important step. Support your request clearly and concisely.

Obtaining a Part-Time Job as an Outsider

Recall our discussion of the three ways you can start work as a part-time professional, either in government or in the private sector:

1. You respond to a vacancy announcement for a part-time professional job and are hired to fill the vacancy.

2. You learn about a vacancy for a full-time professional job, and you convince the hiring official that this job can be performed by you part time.

3. You create your own part-time professional position by persuading a prospective employer that you have something special to offer.

At the federal level, the best strategy for an outsider without career status is to create your own professional position by persuading a federal manager that you have something special to offer. Do not assume that because you see a wonderful federal announcement about a professional position (either part-time or full-time) for which you are well qualified that you can apply and expect to be hired.

Job vacancies at the professional level in the federal government often are restricted to applicants with career status, that is, individuals who have worked for the federal government at least three years. Outsiders usually must have reinstatement eligibility from prior employment. In some cases, only an agency's own employees may apply. One way to enter federal service directly from the outside is to apply for a position with an excepted federal agency, one that is excepted from standard hiring procedures. The Nuclear Regulatory Commission and the Federal Elections Commission are examples of excepted agencies.

Our experience is that local governments are more open to outside hiring at professional levels. This is less true under tight budgetary conditions or when an actual hiring freeze is in place.

Advertised Vacancies

You, the prospective part-time professional, should look at government vacancy announcements for leads about jobs *and* about agencies that use your skills. Hiring agencies do not place individuals on mailing lists to receive all vacancy announcements, but they often will mail a specifically requested announcement or answer questions about particular jobs over the phone. Many government agencies at all levels have codaphones which list vacancy announcements. Call the agency personnel office for the phone number. Once you hear the brief information given on the codaphone you call personnel for details about the job. Listings are changed regularly.

- Federal government

    At the federal level, the Office of Personnel Management does not maintain a central listing of vacancies. Your best bet is to keep in touch with the personnel offices of individual federal agencies on a bi-monthly or monthly basis. This is sufficient because most vacancy announcements list a minimum of three weeks during which applications are accepted.

    Federal Job Information Centers, present in all major cities, provide general information on the federal hiring process. You can find the center nearest you in Appendix C of this book. Although these centers do not maintain copies of individual vacancy announcements, they can give you information on the professional registers in your field and the mid-level register for generalists.

    If you want to work for the federal government as a part-time professional, you must apply for the relevant professional register in your field plus the mid-level register. Your job classification determines which register you must be on. To find your job classification, use the Office of Personnel Management's X-118 QUALIFICATION STANDARDS HANDBOOK FOR WHITE COLLAR POSITIONS UNDER THE GENERAL SCHEDULE. Then prepare an appropriate Standard Form (SF-171)—the government's version of a résumé—to apply for each register.

- State and local governments

Be sure to check with jurisdictions near you for specific policies. Some local governments allow part-timers or job sharers to apply for full-time vacancies; others specify that the job already must be designated as part time. In addition, many local government personnel offices provide extensive services to job hunters including:

1. Analyzing your application and rating you for the classification(s) and grade(s) for which you qualify.

2. Maintaining requests for job information for specific periods of time and notifying you if a job becomes available in your field.

3. Keeping separate files on women, minorities, and older workers and then marketing these individuals to employers as part of affirmative action goals.

State employment commissions are good sources of information on job vacancies in state and local governments. There is usually a separate book or computer listing for professional and/or white-collar jobs. Part-time jobs may be listed separately.

Creating Your Part-Time Job from the Outside

Unlike many private sector employers, the subject of part-time professional employment is not a new one for government officials. In the federal government, each agency has an official program to promote part–time work. As we have seen, many state and local governments also are on record as favoring part-time employment.

As an outsider, use vacancy announcements as leads to find agencies that recruit in your field. When no full-time or part-time vacancies exist, shop around for agencies that already use part-time professionals or that have reputations for innovative personnel policies. Remember, government agencies differ in their flexibility, needs, and management styles.

In your locality, find the operating official in a government agency who manages a program that can use your skills. Convince that manager that you can best fill that need on a part-time schedule. In the federal sector, there is an additional point to know. A vacancy announcement can be written, tailored to your qualifications, and the manager can request your name from the appropriate register. Of course, your name must appear among the three top candidates on that register.

An ongoing problem for part-timers trying to get their first federal job is competing with individuals who have veterans' preferences and others who apply for part-time jobs with the intention of converting to full time as soon as possible. These "bogus" part-timers take reduced-hours jobs and immediately start looking for full-time positions. Managers become convinced that there is no one "out there" really interested in part-time work.

Special Employment Opportunities

Do not overlook other categories of flexible employment in government at all levels which may provide the experience or entering wedge you need. In the federal government, there are many different kinds of permanent employment besides full-time and part-time employment. Other permanent positions are "seasonal," "on-call," and "intermittent" appointments. Temporary appointments also offer special possibilities in federal, state, and local government.

Permanent Employment in the Federal Government

- Seasonal employment. This refers to recurring periods of work lasting less than twelve months each year. You can work on a full-time, part-time, or intermittent schedule and receive the same pay scale and benefits as permanent employees. Most seasonal jobs last at least six months; then you are placed on nonduty/nonpay status for the remainder of the year. Agencies using professionals as seasonal employees are the U.S. Park

Service, the Internal Revenue Service, and passport offices in the State Department. Work here fluctuates seasonally and predictably.

- On-call employment. An on-call employee serves under a permanent appointment but works on an as-needed basis to help meet unpredictable workloads. These employees are eligible for eventual noncompetitive conversion to permanent positions. As an on-call employee, you receive the same pay rates and benefits as full-time employees. A part-time, on-call employee follows all the regulations pertaining to permanent part-timers.

- Intermittent employment. This refers to nonfull-time employment where the employee serves without a regularly scheduled tour of duty. These employees are not eligible for benefits. When an agency schedules an intermittent employee to work for some portion of each week for two consecutive pay periods, the agency must change the employee's status to permanent part time. Then the individual is eligible for prorated benefits.

Temporary Assignments in Federal, State and Local Government

In early 1985, the Office of Personnel Management (OPM) issued a directive encouraging federal agencies to make more "temporary limited appointments" outside the registers to positions at GS-12 and below. Temporary employment is an "extremely important element in a comprehensive staffing policy," said the OPM directive, "and one which is very cost efficient." These people can work any number of hours per week and their services can be extended for up to four years without OPM approval. The use of temporary appointments makes particular sense, according to OPM, in the following situations:

- when operations are being cut back and employment levels are being reduced

- when dealing with workload peaks

- when protecting the jobs of career employees who are serving in activities facing cutbacks.

Temporary appointments are used extensively by state and local governments. Some are short-term assignments—summer jobs with recreation departments, or one-time research projects. Many are temporary in name only. Budget constraints are one reason permanent jobs are disguised as temporary slots. Particularly for newly offered services, projects are funded for a year at a time during evaluation. This process can go on for several years before the job officially becomes permanent.

A second reason is time pressure. To comply with personnel regulations regarding permanent positions, a certain number of candidates must be interviewed at each step of the hiring process. These procedures can take a long time. When urgent needs surface, managers often will request some temporary help. Temporary situations then can turn into permanent jobs.

Very often, temporary positions are not announced officially. You hear about them only through contacts. A manager usually can hire an individual directly, without going through normal hiring procedures. When temporary jobs are converted to permanent status, the job must be opened up to all applicants. As a temporary appointee, you might find yourself competing for your own job. If you have been performing well, it is likely that the job will be yours permanently.

Chapter Eleven

Solving Problems on the Job

Part-time professionals like working reduced hours. Almost unanimously, in a survey of members of the Association of Part-Time Professionals in the Washington, D.C. area, they described themselves as very satisfied or somewhat satisfied with their part-time jobs. By looking at the individuals who are very satisfied with their part-time employment, we can see which employers have the most highly satisfied part-timers:

Table 6.
Very Satisfied Part-Timers
by Types of Employers

	(%)
Nonprofit organizations	61
Federal government	58
State government	53
Self-employed	46
Local government	44
For-profit organizations	40

Why do professionals seek part-time work? Among female respondents to the APTP survey, forty-eight percent checked "parental responsibilities" as the most important reason for working part time. Using their "education, skills, experience" was the second most important reason. Men reported their two most important reasons for working part time as: (1) using their "education, skills, experience," and (2) "more free time to pursue other interests." Among both men and women, the need for additional income was not a major reason for working part time.

Hours and days worked varied for the part-time professionals responding to the APTP survey. Almost two-thirds worked between 20 and 32 hours per week. The most popular schedules were a full day, part week and a part day, part week.

Satisfaction among professionals in part-time jobs does not mean there are no problems on the job. The APTP survey shows what these problems are, and our experience talking and working with part-time professionals over the years confirms the survey results. Although part-timers can readily think of many more disadvantages than advantages to part-time employment, the positive factors of flexibility and additional time far outweigh the problems. We summarize below the problems mentioned by part-time professionals in the APTP survey:

Table 7.
Problems Reported by Part-Time Professionals on the Job*

Problem	Number of Times Mentioned	
Negative Attitudes of Supervisors/Co-Workers		**95**
Commitment to job/seriousness questioned, resentment, lack of trust	60	
Left out by co-workers	35	
Inadequate Compensation		**91**
Lack of benefits	59	
Salary too low	32	
Scheduling		**87**
At work		
Staff does not accept part-time schedule/ refuses to plan accordingly	23	
Lack of continuity in tasks	19	
Communication	16	
Meshing Work/Home Schedules		
Irregular/unpredictable hours	12	
Other	17	
Professional Development/Advancement		**85**
No supervisory responsibilities; no recognition; no special assignments, travel, training; job poorly defined; no access to decisionmakers	27	
Underemployed: work not fulfilling or does not use one's skills	22	
Limited upward mobility, no seniority	21	
No job security	15	
Unrealistic Expectations for Performance		**48**
Full-time results demanded		
No Problems		**42**
Pressure to Work Full Time		**15**

*From 1981 survey of APTP members, Washington Area Chapter

Questioning Your Professional Commitment

You, as a qualified professional, expect to perform effectively on the job. As you move into a part-time slot, others will question your seriousness, your competence, and your loyalty. Be prepared to confront these negative attitudes from supervisors and co-workers. They will arise over matters large and small. For example, one part-time professional tells of the time she almost lost her desk to make room for a summer employee who would be there "full time." All the part-time professionals cited in this book give advice on how to counter these negative attitudes. Briefly stated, you must:

- Show that part–time employment does work and that you are dedicated to the job. Work harder. Be very professional. Take initiative.

- Cultivate rapport with your colleagues and superiors. Meet people in the organization. Communicate and keep in touch.

As one part-time professional put it: "I try to let them know that my job is more important than my schedule, that their objectives are mine and I want to be part of the team." Remember, you are a pioneer. Your effective performance will pave the way for others.

One point should be mentioned about the isolation of part-time professionals—their feeling that they are left out by co-workers. Partly this is a matter of personality. Some professionals want to participate in office socializing. Others do not enjoy it and are glad to have an excuse for avoiding this camaraderie. It is a mistake, we suggest, to avoid all social interaction in the name of "getting the job done." Some informal "chit-chat" and networking with co-workers result in better communication and integration of the part-timer into the work environment.

Inadequate Compensation

Lack of benefits and low salaries are a common problem for all part-time workers, including part-time professionals. Commissioner Thomas Plewes of the Bureau of Labor Statistics discussed the reasons for inadequate compensation at the first National Conference on Part-Time Employment, sponsored by the Association of Part-Time Professionals:

> "Although part-timers earn less than full-timers because they work fewer hours, it is also true, but less obvious, that on an average, part-timers earn considerably less per hour than do their full-time counterparts. This wage gap arises less because employers pay part-timers a lower rate for the same work (though many do), than because part-timers seem to be relegated to lower paid sectors. In addition, part-time workers are concentrated in occupations noted for fast worker turnover. Jobs with fast turnovers are infamous for low wages and difficult working conditions, with a lesser investment in labor training and fringe benefits than other jobs."

The survey of APTP members reported earlier found that only two out of five part-timers received some type of standard benefits. The most common benefit was vacation leave; the least common was life insurance. Consider the figures below for details:

Table 8.
Selected Benefits
Received by Part-Time Personnel, 1981

	Benefits	No Benefits
Life Insurance	64 (22%)	231 (78%)
Health Insurance	87 (29%)	207 (71%)
Retirement	85 (29%)	210 (71%)
Sick Leave	116 (39%)	179 (61%)
Vacation Leave	122 (41%)	173 (59%)

The federal government appears to be the most generous employer in the area of benefits to part-time workers. There is a startling disparity between the federal government and nonfederal employers in the benefits they accord to part-timers. The following table tells the story:

Table 9.
Part-Timers Receiving Selected Benefits by Types of Employers, 1981

	Federal Govt. (%)	State Govt. (%)	Local Govt. (%)	Nonprofit Orgs. (%)	For-Profit Orgs. (%)	Other (%)	
Life Insurance (Recipients = 64)	64	2	16	5	14	–	= 100%
Health Insurance (Recipients = 87)	59	5	9	10	15	2	= 100%
Retirement (Recipients = 85)	69	4	6	14	27	–	= 100%
Sick Leave (Recipients = 116)	58	2	8	18	13	1	= 100%
Vacation Leave (Recipients = 122)	56	1	8	20	14	1	= 100%

Results of the APTP survey merely confirm the fact that the federal government has been a leader in providing part-timers with prorated pay and benefits. It would be wise for you, as a prospective part-time professional, to use the federal structure of benefits as a guide in your negotiations with private employers. You should know that part-timers working for the federal government enjoy the following benefits:

- Pay. Gross basic pay is computed by multiplying the hourly rate of pay by the number of hours worked during the pay period. The grade level is determined by difficulty of work and is not affected by the number of hours the employee works.

- Overtime. Overtime or compensatory time is given to eligible part-time employees working more than eight hours a day, or forty hours per week. Working more than a normal part-time schedule does not entitle you to overtime.

- Schedules. Part-timers work from sixteen to thirty-two hours weekly. Precise schedules are determined by the employee and supervisor.

- Leave. Annual and sick leave accrue on a prorated basis.

- Holidays. Part-timers receive all holidays which fall on normally scheduled work days.

- Health insurance. Part-time and full-time employees receive the same coverage. The part-timer pays the employee's share of the premium plus a prorated portion of the employer's share.

- Life insurance. Both group life and optional insurance are available to part-timers. The amount of coverage is based on salary, with a minimum coverage of $10,000.

- Retirement. Retirement benefits are computed in the same way for all career employees. Annuities are based on an employee's length of service and the highest annual basic pay received for any three consecutive years.

- Credits for years of service. A full year of credit is given for each calendar year to compute a part-timer's service for tenure, retirement, promotion, and other requirements.

- Appeal rights. Part-time and full-time personnel have the same appeal rights in adverse actions. A manager's decision to increase a part-time employee's schedule is not an adverse action subject to appeal.

Employers are more likely to provide benefits if part-time professionals

- speak up

- press hard enough

- are accepted as competent permanent members of the organization's work force, and

- can present a written proposal showing how prorated benefits do not cost the employer additional money (review Chapter Seven for details). Karen Hardiman and Paula Eiblum provide evidence of action by part-timers to advance the cause of prorated benefits. You can follow their stories below.

Karen Hardiman
Librarian, City of National City, CA

Karen Hardiman works twenty hours per week for this California municipality as a reference librarian. She filed a grievance because benefits and salary advances for part-time employees were not spelled out in the existing Memorandum of Understanding between the City of National City and the Employees' Association. Ms. Hardiman's whole purpose in using the grievance procedure was to raise a series of questions which needed answers.

Although Karen Hardiman lost her grievance case (the Civil Service Commission decided it was not a "grievable" issue), she won the war. The benefits and salary sections of the official Memorandum of Understanding were renegotiated bringing, she says, "a fair, even-handed recognition of part-time employees."

Now, permanent part-time employees in the competitive service receive every benefit earned by full-time employees, prorated at fifty percent. Moreover, they earn benefits in the same number of months as full-time people. Salary increases, for example, come after twelve months for full- and part-time staff.

On health, dental, and life insurance the amount paid by the city for each permanent part-time employee is proportional to the permanent time base of his/her appointment. A person working half-time, for example, receives one-half the payment of a full-time employee.

Paula Eiblum
Project Director, Capital Systems Group, Washington, D.C.

Paula Eiblum provides another example of a part-time professional struggling successfully for expanded benefit coverage. Her company, an information services firm, always gave medical insurance and profit sharing to company employees working thirty hours or more per week. Now, thanks to Paula, Capital Systems Group also offers prorated holidays and vacations.

Originally hired in 1980 as an information specialist, Ms. Eiblum worked a sixteen–hour week for the firm. Gradually, her responsibilities grew and her work schedule increased to thirty-plus hours. At the same time, she became increasingly upset about the lack of paid vacations and holidays. So she decided to act. As new managers took over, Paula Eiblum alerted them to the outstanding loyalty, effectiveness, and commitment of the firm's part-timers. In addition, she pressed the case for prorated benefits with the company's personnel director.

The outcome was positive. The firm granted prorated holidays and vacations for part-timers working more than thirty hours weekly. Also, Paula Eiblum became director of Info-Quest, a subsidiary project of Capital Systems Group, doing information research, data-base searching, and document delivery.

Some conclusions from Paula Eiblum's success: top work skills, pride in being a part-time professional, and self-confidence in talking with management about inequities do pay off!

Scheduling at Work and Home

Part-time professionals confront complex scheduling issues when they work reduced hours. Meshing with colleagues' schedules, communicating, and maintaining continuity in job tasks are all issues that must be faced. Some good advice comes from APTP members holding part-time jobs:

- Speak with employers and co-workers frequently to clarify schedules and role in the organization.

- Be very organized and efficient. Plan ahead.

- Improve communication. Write notes. Attend all meetings. Keep others informed about the status of your work. A weekly calendar posted on your door or on a chalkboard is a good way to let colleagues know when you are in. Project status sheets placed in convenient spots is another good communications tool.

Contradictory advice often is given about flexibility and firmness in adhering to part-time schedules. How flexible should you be in breaking your schedule to come in for a special meeting or during a crisis? When do you say, "No?" Should you take work home? How available must you be for phone calls? How are you compensated for extra time? All these issues are subject to negotiation when you enter the job or after an initial period of time on the job. Do not hesitate to bring up scheduling issues with your boss because they will affect your performance. Here are some rules of thumb:

1. Occasionally, change your schedule, but do not let this become a habit. Part-time professionals must respond to occasional crises by staying late or going to work on an off-day. Preferably, such situations can be dealt with over the phone from home. Support staff are crucial here to alert you to crises and to work with you at solving them from home.
   Breaking your schedule to attend to constant crises means your status as a part-timer is impaired.

Colleagues will start expecting you to be available throughout the work week. If important activities—staff meetings, for example—regularly are scheduled during your off time, either rearrange your schedule to attend these meetings, or take the initiative to change these meetings to your work days.

2. Constant overtime at the office or at home should be compensated. If you start working longer hours regularly due to job pressures, ask for additional compensation. Consider a part-time version of flexi–time. Try to establish a base period of hours and days you work and a range of availability outside these hours, with appropriate compensation for the base and for the extra time. Also monitor your at-home work. When at-home work starts mounting up to one-half day per week, renegotiate your salary to compensate for this.

3. Remind people at home that you are employed in a professional capacity. Especially for a female with family responsibilities, a part-time career may be perceived as the equivalent of being at home full time. Do not overestimate the amount of time you can devote to household chores or to community activities. After all, a part-time professional position is a demanding one with constant pressure to perform well. Reduce your workload at home and in the community to accommodate your job schedule.

Professional Development and Advancement

Unchallenging work and limited promotion opportunities are repeatedly cited by part-time professionals as problems on the job. Although numerous APTP members are part-time managers and supervisors, most employers rate these positions as off-limits for part-timers.

Ask for more challenging assignments or special training. Employers may not recognize that you, as a part-time professional, want to go the extra mile for career advancement. Remember that the stereotype of the less serious, uncommitted professional must be overcome, so it is important to push for professional development and advancement.

Full-Time Results Demanded

Many full-time professional jobs can be done on a reduced work schedule. You may be sufficiently competent and well-organized—and the full-time job may have sufficient slack in it—to make this a realistic option. If the existing full-time job is genuinely a forty to fifty hour a week job you have two options in converting it to part time:

1. Separate out tasks that are impossible for you to accomplish and have them assigned to another worker, or

2. Create a job sharing situation where two partners will share responsibility, each part time, for a single job.

Trying to fill a bona fide full-time job on a reduced work schedule only brings grief. The employer will press you for full-time performance. You will work overtime extensively at home and/or the office. You will feel constant stress. In effect, you will be getting part-time pay for a full-time job. Do not do it!

Employer Pressure to Work Full Time

This pressure usually means that your work is highly regarded, there is a lot to do in your job, and your employer wishes she/he could employ you on a full-time basis. Evaluate your career situation carefully. Are you planning to return to full-time work? If so, when? Once you clarify your own personal and career goals, talk to your employer. Provide a target date for your conversion to full time, or frankly tell the employer that you intend to work part time for the foreseeable future.

Full discussion of your intentions with your employer may relieve the pressures on you to work full time. It may lead to a rearrangement of your work responsibilities so you and your employer can be satisfied with your part-time schedule.

Chapter Twelve

The Future is Yours

You now know that the part-time professional option is not a fairy tale. Good jobs exist in different professions, some with managerial responsibilities.

"What about the future?" After all, obtaining part-time professional positions will be easier if the work place generally is moving in that direction. Our answer is that employers will be more receptive to part-time professionals in the future. Growth has occurred in the 1970's; it will continue into the 1980's and 1990's for many reasons.

Demand for Part-Time Professional Jobs

More professionally trained, career minded women are in the job market than ever before. They want flexible work schedules, particularly to assist in meeting family responsibilities. Women outnumber men as new entrants into the work force by two to one, and the fastest growing segment of the labor force is women with children under six. These women seek to use their professional skills and retain primary responsibility for child care. The solution for many young mothers is a reduced work schedule.

As the population ages, we will see more older professionals. Many wish to augment their retirement incomes and to use their experience and knowledge on a less than full-time basis. Others would prefer to phase down into retirement. The rising cost to private pension systems and Social Security of early retirement is just being recognized by government and business. The nation cannot afford policies which encourage early retirement and discourage post-retirement employment, especially when older people are living longer and healthier lives. Moreover, predictions are for shortages of young people in the work force by the 1990's, reenforcing the need to keep skilled older people on the job. More part-time opportunities for qualified older workers will be an urgent requirement.

Increasing numbers of professional women with children and of retired professionals are speaking up to make the case for part-time employment. In professional organizations—for example, the American Bar Association—committees of female professionals are asking for action on part–time employment and other family and work place issues. The Association of Part-Time Professionals, a national organization of part-timers, also reflects the trend toward increased assertiveness by men and women who want part-time opportunities.

Many employers still are not aware of the need for part-time employment, especially at professional levels. A survey of part-time policies and practices at large firms conducted by the National Council for Alternative Work Patterns in 1984 found relatively little interest in part time, but expectations of increased usage in the future. Employers were surprised by the low demand, reports Gail Rosenberg, council president, but they conceded that workers might not want to cut back during a time of scarce jobs.

A vicious circle operates on the part-time issue. Employers perceive a lack of interest in part time so there are few part-time openings. Since there are few part-time openings, especially at professional levels, workers feel discouraged and do not believe part time is a possibility. The point is to crack the vicious circle. Most often, the first breakthrough occurs when a valued employee negotiates reduced hours, establishing a precedent for part-time work.

Supply of Part-Time Professional Jobs

Many employers are finding it cost effective to employ part-time professionals—you met some of them in Chapter Three. As managers and employees witness successful use of part time, there are more requests for reduced hours and more willingness by employers to experiment. These positive experiences are accumulating and more part-time professional opportunities are opening up.

But, change takes time. The world of work still is adjusting to the dramatic societal changes of the past twenty years. Most corporate executives do not consider meeting society's needs as a primary business concern. Yet when these needs burst forth in concrete situations—for example, losing experienced female managers who are having babies—companies do respond. It is, after all, good business to keep excellent employees.

In the future, according to Helen Axel of The Conference Board, firms will be more responsive to internal and external demands for flexible work hours. Part time now is firmly established in certain industries—banking and insurance, for example—but beyond these industries, decisions are made on a case-by-case basis. Changes in the nature of industry are facilitating work place shifts, Ms. Axel concludes, because they "disturb traditional patterns of doing business" and "encourage a climate for innovative planning that seeks to make optimum use of human and other resources." She calls these changes the four "D's":

- **Decentralization and Diversification.** They favor local autonomy in decision–making and a more flexible approach by management.

- **Deregulation.** This forces firms to be more market responsive and more competitive.

- **Down sizing.** This promotes a trimmer work force and better use of personnel.

Again, change takes time! American managers often cling to traditional attitudes and practices. Part-time professional employment, for these managers, is a contradiction in terms. Even among companies with sizeable numbers of professionals on reduced hours, part-timers often are set apart from the full-time permanent work force. Viewed as buffers, with little job security, the part-timers sometimes do not receive prorated benefits. These practices may change as more companies review their policies on part-time employment.

Impending shortages of skilled labor can be persuasive factors in motivating employers to accept reduced work schedules for professionals. Falling birth rates may yield labor shortages in many fields by the 1990's. When the labor supply tightens up, employers are more willing to work with employees to juggle work schedules.

It Is Up To You

Wishing will not make it so. If you want part-time professional employment, you must act. Professionals today are requesting and obtaining part-time schedules. American employers today are awakening to the advantages of professionals working shorter hours. Progress is steady and sure.

Weigh the pros and cons of a part-time professional job. Decide whether time and flexibility mean more to you than a reduced paycheck. If you opt for the part-time route, take heart. You need not wait for the world to change. All you require is that one right job for you.

You can join the growing ranks of part-time professionals by seriously and aggressively pursuing the possibilities in your own community. Inform yourself about the part-time option, particularly its impact on employers. Plug into all local networks that might be useful in providing job leads. Be patient and do not become discouraged. You are a pioneer, and you will succeed.

Appendix A

Top Ten Jobs

Appendix A

Top Ten Jobs

1980	1981	1982	1983	1984
1. Teacher	1. Writer	1. Teacher	1. Mental Health Counselor	1. Librarian
2. Librarian	2. Teacher	2. Librarian	2. Computer Programmer	2. Personnel Specialist, Teacher
3. Computer Programmer	3. Mental Health Counselor	3. Writer	3. Librarian	3. Computer Programmer
4. Social Worker	4. Social Worker	4. Social Worker	4. Social Worker	4. Editor, Social Worker
5. Editor	5. Psychologist	5. Editor	5. Nurse, Community Health Educator	5. Writer, Mental Health Counselor
6. Writer, Management Analyst	6. Editor	6. Mental Health Counselor	6. Editor	6. Accountant
7. Program Analyst, Librarian, Psychologist	7. Systems Analyst, Fundraiser	7. Public Relations Specialist, Accountant	7. Writer	7. Nurse, Community Health Educator, Systems Analyst
8. Community Organizer	8. Legislative Affairs Specialist	8. Graphic Artist	8. Accountant	8. Social Science Researcher
9. Mental Health Counselor	9. Management Analyst	9. Clinical Psychologist	9. Psychologist	9. Graphic Artist, Human Services Administrator
10. Accountant	10. Occupational Therapist, Librarian, Graphic Artist, Personnel Specialist	10. Human Services Administrator, Computer Programmer, Technical Writer	10. Teacher	10. Career/Guidance Counselor

Source: Association of Part-Time Professionals Job Referral Service, Washington, D.C. area.
Note: More than one job listed per number indicates a tie.

Appendix B

Unemployment Insurance Taxes by State

Appendix B

Unemployment Insurance Taxes by State

State	1984 Tax Base	1984 Est. Avg. Tax Rate	State	1984 Tax Base	1984 Est. Avg. Tax Rate
Alabama	$ 8,000	2.5%	Montana	$ 8,400	3.1%
Alaska	21,400	2.6	Nebraska	7,000	1.9
Arizona	7,000	1.9	Nevada	10,700	2.8
Arkansas	7,500	3.9	New Hampshire	7,000	1.5
California	7,000	3.3	New Jersey	9,600	3.1
Colorado	8,000	2.7	New Mexico	9,800	1.9
Connecticut	7,100	2.7	New York	7,000	3.2
Delaware	8,000	3.6	North Carolina	8,200	2.1
Dist. of Columbia	8,000	3.0	North Dakota	10,400	3.6
Florida	7,000	1.5	Ohio	8,000	4.8
Georgia	7,000	1.7	Oklahoma	7,000	2.1
Hawaii	14,600	1.9	Oregon	13,000	3.1
Idaho	14,400	3.4	Pennsylvania	8,000	5.3
Illinois	8,000	4.5	Rhode Island	10,000	4.1
Indiana	7,000	2.4	South Carolina	7,000	2.1
Iowa	10,400	3.2	South Dakota	7,000	1.6
Kansas	8,000	2.9	Tennessee	7,000	3.2
Kentucky	8,000	3.7	Texas	7,000	1.6
Louisiana	7,000	3.9	Utah	13,300	3.1
Maine	7,000	3.7	Vermont	8,000	3.3
Maryland	7,000	2.9	Virginia	7,000	2.4
Massachusetts	7,000	3.0	Washington	12,000	3.3
Michigan	8,500	5.5	West Virginia	8,000	4.2
Minnesota	9,800	2.8	Wisconsin	9,500	4.7
Mississippi	7,000	2.8	Wyoming	9,525	3.9
Missouri	7,000	2.6			

Source: U.S. Department of Labor, Employment and Training Administration

Appendix C

Federal Job Information Centers By State

ALABAMA
Huntsville:
Southerland Building
806 Governors Dr., S.W. 35801
(205) 453-5070

ALASKA
Anchorage:
Federal Bldg.
701 C St., Box 22, 99513
(907) 271-5821

ARIZONA
Phoenix:
U.S. Postal Service Building
522 N. Central Ave. 85004
(602) 261-4736

ARKANSAS
Little Rock:
Federal Bldg., Third Floor
700 W. Capitol Ave. 72201
(501) 378-5842

CALIFORNIA
Los Angeles:
Linder Bldg.
845 S. Figueroa 90017
(213) 688-3360
Sacramento:
1029 J St., Rm. 202 95814
(916) 440-3441
San Diego:
880 Front St. 92188
(714) 293-6165
San Francisco:
211 Main St.,
Second Floor 94105
(415) 974-9725

COLORADO
Denver:
1845 Sherman St. 80203
(303) 837-3509

CONNECTICUT
Hartford:
Federal Bldg., Rm. 613,
450 Main St. 06103
(203) 722-3096

DISTRICT OF COLUMBIA
Metro Area:
  1900 E Street, N.W., 20415
  (202) 737-9616

FLORIDA
Orlando:
  Federal Bldg. and
  U.S. Courthouse
  80 N. Hughey Ave. 32801
  (305) 420-6148 or 6149

GEORGIA
Atlanta:
  Richard B. Russell Federal
  Bldg., 9th Floor
  75 Spring St. SW, 30303
  (404) 221-4315

GUAM
Agana:
  Pacific News Bldg.
  238 O'Hara St.
  Room 308 96910
  344-5242

HAWAII
Honolulu (and Island of Oahu):
  Federal Bldg., Room 1310
  300 Ala Moana Blvd. 96850
  (808) 546-8600

ILLINOIS
Chicago:
  55 E. Jackson, Room 1401
  60604
  (312) 353-5136

INDIANA
Indianapolis:
  46 East Ohio Street,
  Room 124, 46204
  (317) 269-7161

IOWA
Des Moines:
  210 Walnut St., Rm. 191, 50309
  (515) 284-4545
In Scott and Pottawattamie
Counties dial (402) 221-3815

KANSAS
Wichita:
  One-Twenty Bldg., Rm. 101
  120 S. Market St. 67202
  (316) 269-6106
In Johnson, Leavenworth and
Wyandotte Counties dial
(816) 374-5702

LOUISIANA
New Orleans:
  F. Edward Hebert Bldg.
  610 South St., Rm. 849 70130
  (504) 589-2764

MARYLAND
Baltimore:
  Garmatz Federal Building
  101 W. Lombard St., 21201
  (301) 962-3822
DC Metro Area:
  1900 E St. N.W., 20415
  (202) 737-9616

MASSACHUSETTS
Boston:
  3 Center Plaza, 02108
  (617) 223-2571

MICHIGAN
Detroit:
  477 Michigan Ave.
  Rm. 565, 48226
  (313) 226-6950

MINNESOTA
Twin Cities:
  Federal Bldg.
  Ft. Snelling, Twin Cities. 55111
  (612) 725-4430

MISSISSIPPI
Jackson:
  100 W. Capitol St.
  (Suite 335) 39260
  (601) 960-4585

MISSOURI
Kansas City:
Federal Bldg., Rm. 134
601 E. 12th St. 64106
(816) 374-5702
St. Louis:
Old Post Office, Rm. 400
815 Olive St. 63101
(314) 425-4285

NEBRASKA
Omaha:
U.S. Courthouse and
Post Office Bldg.
Rm. 1010, 215 N. 17th St.
68102
(402) 221-3815

NEW HAMPSHIRE
Portsmouth:
Thomas J. McIntyre Federal
Bldg., Rm. 104
80 Daniel Street, 03801
(603) 436-7220 ext. 762

NEW JERSEY
Newark:
Peter W. Rodino, Jr.,
Federal Bldg.
970 Broad St. 07102
(201) 645-3673
In Camden, dial (215) 597-7440

NEW MEXICO
Albuquerque:
Federal Bldg.
421 Gold Ave. SW. 87102
(505) 766-5583

NEW YORK
New York City:
Jacob K. Javits Federal Bldg.
26 Federal Plaza, 10278
(212) 264-0422
Syracuse:
James N. Hanley Federal Bldg.
100 S. Clinton St. 13260
(315) 423-5660

NORTH CAROLINA
Raleigh:
Federal Bldg.
310 New Bern Ave.
P.O. Box 25069, 27611
(919) 755-4361

OHIO
Dayton:
Federal Building
200 W 2nd St., 45402
(513) 225-2720

OKLAHOMA
Oklahoma City:
200 NW Fifth St.,
Rm. 205, 73102
(405) 231-4948

OREGON
Portland:
Federal Bldg.
1220 SW Third St., 97204
(503) 221-3141

PENNSYLVANIA
Harrisburg:
Federal Bldg., Rm. 168, 17108
(717) 782-4494
Philadelphia:
Wm. J. Green, Jr., Fed. Bldg.
600 Arch Street, 19106
(215) 597-7440
Pittsburgh:
Fed. Bldg.
1000 Liberty Ave., 15222
(412) 644-2755

PUERTO RICO
San Juan:
Federico Degetau Federal Bldg.
Carlos E. Chardon St.
Hato Rey, P.R. 00918
(809) 753-4209

RHODE ISLAND
Providence:
John O. Pastori Federal Bldg.
Rm. 310
Kennedy Plaza 02903
(401) 528-5251

SOUTH CAROLINA
Charleston:
  Federal Bldg.,
  334 Meeting St., 29403
  (803) 724-4328

TENNESSEE
Memphis:
  100 N. Main St.,
  Suite 1312 38103
  (901) 521-3956

TEXAS
Dallas:
  Rm. 6B4,
  1100 Commerce St., 75242
  (214) 767-8035
Houston:
  701 San Jacinto St.,
  4th Floor. 77002
  (713) 226-2375
San Antonio:
  643 E. Durango Blvd., 78206
  (512) 229-6611

VIRGINIA
Norfolk:
  Federal Bldg., Rm. 220.
  200 Granby Mall. 23510
  (804) 441-3355
D.C. Metro Area:
  1900 E Street, N.W. 20415
  (202) 737-9616

WASHINGTON
Seattle:
  Federal Bldg.,
  915 Second Ave. 98174
  (206) 442-4365

WEST VIRGINIA
Charleston:
  Federal Bldg.,
  500 Quarrier St. 25301
  (304) 343-6181, ext. 226

Appendix D

Association of Part-Time Professionals

The ASSOCIATION OF PART-TIME PROFESSIONALS, INC. is a nonprofit membership organization promoting part-time employment opportunities for professional men and women. Starting with a successful local group in the Washington, D.C. area, APTP is expanding throughout the country. APTP works to:

- upgrade the status of part-time employment by providing a professional association that represents, and speaks for, all part-time professionals—permanent part-timers, job sharers, free lancers, and consultants;

- educate employers, employees, and the community about the advantages of increased flexibility in working patterns;

- advocate prorated benefits for part-timers and a work environment responsive to individual and family needs;

- organize a constituency of professional men and women nationwide who want the part-time employment option available to them.

For further information, write to:
Association of Part-Time Professionals
P.O. Box 3419
Alexandria, VA 22302
(703) 734-7975

Appendix E

Your Experiences as a Part-Time Professional

Please take a few moments to fill out this brief questionnaire. We want your feedback for the next edition of this book.

Your name_____

Address_____ Zip_____

Phone (   )_____(H) (   )_____(O)

Current occupation_____

Are you seeking part-time employment? ☐ Yes ☐ No

Are you currently employed? ☐ Yes ☐ No

If currently employed, do you work part time? ☐ Yes
☐ No

If you are currently employed on a part-time basis,

Name of employer_____

How did you obtain your part-time position?_____

_____

_____

_____

_____

How satisfied are you with your part-time position?

☐ very satisfied
☐ somewhat satisfied
☐ not at all satisfied

What is the biggest problem you face as a part-timer?_____

_____

_____

_____

_____

What topics particularly helped you in this book?_____

_____

_____

_____

What additional information would you like to see included
in the next edition?

_____

_____

_____

_____

THANK YOU. Please return to:

APTP
PO Box 3419
Alexandria, VA 22302

Index

Rehabilitation/Vocational counselor, 108
Research occupations, 17, 19, 109
Rosenberg, Gail, 138

S

San Antonio College, 27, 28
San Francisco, CA, 109
Schroeder, Pat, 47
Social insurance administrator, 105
Social science analyst, 106
Social Security, 82
Social worker, 16, 17, 44, 109
Speech therapist, 109
Statistician, 65, 106
Sterling Systems, 78
Substance abuse counselor, 109
Systems analyst, 17, 39, 106, 109

T

Technician, 15, 44
Teacher, 15, 16, 17, 27, 103, 109
Trainer, 109
Travelers Insurance Companies, 42
Trust officer, 42

U

Underwriter, 43
Unemployment Insurance, 83
U.S. Commission on Civil Rights, 64
U.S. Department of Agriculture, 19
U.S. Department of Education, 64, 65
University of Texas, 27, 28
Urban planner, 109

V

Veterans Administration, 64, 65
Volunteer coordinator, 109

W

Wichita, KS, 109
Women's Work Project, 30
Workers' Compensation, 84
Writer, 16, 17, 30, 39, 109